through
the EYES
of another

Hay House Titles of Related Interest

through
the EYES
of another

*A Medium's Guide
to Creating Heaven on Earth by
Encountering Your Life Review Now*

Karen Noe

HAY HOUSE, INC.
Carlsbad, California • New York City
London • Sydney • Johannesburg
Vancouver • Hong Kong • New Delhi

Published and distributed in the United States by: Hay House, Inc.:
www.hayhouse.com* • **Published and distributed in Australia by:** Hay
House Australia Pty. Ltd.: www.hayhouse.com.au • **Published and distributed in the United Kingdom by:** Hay House UK, Ltd.: www.hayhouse
.co.uk • **Published and distributed in the Republic of South Africa by:**
Hay House SA (Pty), Ltd.: www.hayhouse.co.za • **Distributed in Canada
by:** Raincoast: www.raincoast.com • **Published in India by:** Hay House
Publishers India: www.hayhouse.co.in

Cover design: Amy Rose Grigoriou • *Interior design:* Riann Bender

Previously published by Balboa Press (ISBN: 978-145250-150-5)

Library of Congress Cataloging-in-Publication Data

Noe, Karen.
  Through the eyes of another : a medium's guide to creating heaven on
earth by encountering your life review now / by Karen Lazzarini Noe.
-- 1st ed.
      p. cm.
  ISBN 978-1-4019-4014-0 (trade pbk. : alk. paper)
  1.   Interpersonal communication. 2.   Autobiography--Psychological
aspects. 3. Letter writing--Psychological aspects. 4. Interpersonal rela-
tions--Psychological aspects. 5. Interpersonal relations--Psychic aspects.
6. Peace of mind. I. Title.
  BF637.C45N6145 2012
  133.9'1--dc23
                                      2012012925

Tradepaper ISBN: 978-1-84850-969-6

15 14 13 12   4 3 2 1
1st edition, July 2012

This book is dedicated to my three precious angels,
the loves of my life, Chris, Jessica, and Tim.
You are everything a mother could ever want
and more. I'm so proud of each one of you,
and I love you so very much!

contents

preface

As a medium, I don't *believe* the soul is eternal; I *know* it, just as I know I am typing these words right now. I have seen tremendous, peaceful transformations in my clients after they received definite messages from their deceased loved ones telling them they are okay. In my first book, *The Rainbow Follows the Storm: How to Obtain Inner Peace by Connecting with Angels and Deceased Loved Ones*, I discuss this in much more detail, but the essential point is this: your soul is energy. When that energy leaves your body after physical death, its essence will continue. Many years of communicating with those who have crossed over to the other side has enabled me to come to this definite conclusion.

Several years ago, I began receiving consistent messages from angels and deceased loved ones after going through a difficult time in my life. One day, as

I was sitting on the corner of my bed with my head in my hands, I asked God and the angels if I was going to be all right. Within a few seconds, I saw a beautiful golden light coming toward me from the other side of the room. My first reaction was to declare, "If you are not of God, please leave!" However, even after I said this, the magnificent light continued to float toward me.

The light entered the top of my head and eventually enveloped me. At that time, an incredible peace came upon me, and I began to weep. During this experience, I felt completely at one with God, the angels, and everyone else. I continued to cry, and soon I heard an audible voice speaking to me: "Luce lucina, bella luce lucina." Thank goodness my grandparents were Italian, so I knew what that meant: "Light, little light, beautiful little light." After hearing these words, I breathed a sigh of relief as I experienced each of my so-called problems being lifted from me one by one. Although I was totally unaware of it at the time, this incident became a huge turning point in my life. I had been given the most incredible gift, and I would never be the same again.

This whole experience changed not only *my* life, but also the lives of those around me. I began to experience a peacefulness and tranquility that I had

never felt before, and I had an inner knowingness about things that I was unable to understand previously. Whereas, before, I had been searching for angels, now I *knew* them. Whereas, before, I had heard about the oneness of everyone, now I *felt* this link to everyone and everything.

My psychic abilities also increased dramatically. In the beginning, the messages I received from angels and departed loved ones started off slowly and then occurred more frequently. At first I didn't want to share these messages with others because I didn't want people to think I wasn't in my right mind, but when I gave in and shared these messages, I saw just how much peace it provided everyone. These messages from deceased loved ones were all very specific, so that their living loved ones knew without a doubt that what was coming through was real.

I finally gave in and rented space by the hour in the back of a hair salon to provide Reiki healings, and it was just an added benefit if someone "came through" from the spirit world. I'll never forget one of the first readings I ever did, which was for a young woman named Jill, who had come to see me on the recommendation of both her mother and grandmother. After doing a healing on her and receiving messages from her grandfather, I saw a car in my mind's eye. On the side of the car, I saw what I thought couldn't possibly mean anything to her: a kangaroo with boxing gloves. I was reluctant to tell her what I had received because it seemed so strange, yet a male figure in the spirit world kept pushing me to tell her what he had shown me. When I finally broke down and told her, she gasped and said, "Yes, that's my friend Rob. He died in a car accident . . . and he boxed kangaroos in Australia."

After that appointment, I finally realized without a doubt that I was receiving real messages from those who had crossed over. After all, I couldn't possibly have known that about her friend. I continued to receive specific, sometimes-crazy messages from deceased loved ones. Word started to spread, and I eventually needed to rent my own space. Suddenly, I was booked for months ahead of time, and my client list grew and grew to the point where, now, twelve years later, I am booked over a year and a half ahead of time, and have to turn down new clients due to the overwhelming demand for appointments from my current ones.

I am sharing all of this with you to show you who I am and why I am able to speak so freely about what a soul goes through after physical death. Although the majority of this book is not about the

messages I have received from departed loved ones, which was covered in my first book, I did include in the appendix of this book stories from some of my favorite readings so that you can fully understand a very important fact: life does not end after physical death; it just continues!

introduction

As a medium, I often hear regrets from those who have crossed over to the other side that they "should have" or "could have" said or done certain things while they were still here. Unfortunately, at this point, the only way they feel they can communicate these unspoken words to their loved ones is through a medium, like myself.

Likewise, people who come into my office often say they never told loved ones they were trying to contact just how much they really loved or appreciated them. Because of things left unsaid or undone, they also have many regrets.

After hearing this over and over again, I began to wonder how our lives would be different if we were to tell our loved ones how much they meant to us right now, while they are still here with us. I just knew this would be life changing!

Therefore, I decided to conduct an experiment. I asked clients who were interested in participating to write different types of letters to important people in their lives and, if they felt guided, to mail or hand these letters to the recipients. Because I was highly motivated to make amends with loved ones in my own life, I participated in this experiment as well. The results were better than I ever could have imagined.

In Part I of this book, I talk about what a life review is and explain the benefits of doing a life review now, instead of waiting until we cross over to see the "bigger picture." I explain how we can use letters as a platform for going through this life review, and I focus on how my life changed for the better after I had written various types of letters to myself and my own living and deceased loved ones.

In Part II, I discuss the different types of letters you can write to yourself and to your loved ones, and show you how you can go through the whole process of creating peace in your life by seeing through the eyes of others. As an added bonus in this part, I include a chapter on how you can receive messages and get signs from your deceased loved ones, and I explain how to find a good medium if you feel that you are not receiving such signs.

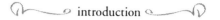

In Part III, I explain why it is important to maintain the peace you have created with your loved ones long after your letters have been written, and discuss why you should continue to honor and love yourself as well. I also show you that inner peace does not come from a change in circumstances; it comes from a change in your *perception* of them.

Finally, in the Appendix, I share some of my favorite stories from readings that answer questions my clients often ask me concerning the afterlife and more. You can even go to this section first if you wish, because it stands on its own.

So read on to find out how to see the "bigger picture," that is, how to see everything through the eyes of others. When you are able to accomplish this, you and every person in your life will feel loved, honored, and respected. In other words, you will be creating heaven right here on earth for you and for those around you.

※ ◎ ※

the
JOURNEY—
my personal
life review

CHAPTER 1

encountering the life review now

Your spirit continues to exist after the physical body dies. When you make your transition, you will feel exactly how you have affected all your loved ones, through their eyes. This *life review* will be a way of understanding the impact you had on others during your earthly existence. During a life review, which is also sometimes called a *panoramic life review,* you will instantly become everyone you have encountered. Whatever you did or didn't do to others you will experience as if it had been done or not done to you. (If you are interested in reading more on this topic, I highly recommend a wonderful book called *Saved by the Light,* by Dannion Brinkley, in which the author describes his near-death experience after he had been struck by lightning and declared clinically dead for 28 minutes. He discusses his life review in detail and how it forever changed him.)

Why Do a Life Review While We Are Still Here?

As I stated in the Introduction, deceased people are sometimes frustrated because they feel that it's now too late for them to make amends with their living loved ones. After hearing this over and over, I began to wonder what would happen if we could encounter our life review while we were still here on earth. I just knew that it would create so much peace—in not only *our* lives but also the lives of those around us—if we really were able to see how our actions have affected others. It would give us the perfect opportunity to identify what we need to change to "get it right" *before* we make our transition.

Then, if we took it a step further and did whatever was necessary to make these changes, we'd be able to release so much unwanted guilt, resentment, and shame. We'd finally be able to get rid of negative attachments to our past while creating more harmonious relationships in the present.

Our loved ones would enjoy being around us and would no longer feel frustrated about not being heard. They would be able to see how much we

really do love them, and sense how much we want to maintain this newfound peace with them.

Writing Letters as a Platform for the Life Review

After asking the angels to show me how I could go through my life review now, they immediately brought to my attention a letter-writing exercise that my children had been given when they were going through the process of receiving the sacrament of confirmation. Parents and siblings were told to write letters to their children, telling them how much they loved and appreciated them.

I remembered what a wonderful opportunity it had been to tell my children how special they were and just how much I admired all of their amazing, unique qualities. It had been such a positive experience for all of us. As an awesome surprise, after I had written my letters to my children, they each wrote one back to me as well. To this day, we return to these precious letters whenever we need to be reminded that we are truly loved.

After I started reminiscing about this experience, it suddenly dawned on me why the angels had brought this exercise to my attention: This type of letter writing would be such a wonderful way of telling our loved ones how much they meant to us now! It's so simple! We could just sit down and write everything we would want our loved ones to know, as if we were looking back at our lives with them. The letter would be a very positive one—one that would make them feel good. In this letter, we would tell them everything we cherished about them, making sure to include anything that we would regret not saying after we left this world.

If there were loved ones in our lives with whom we had regrets, a letter-writing exercise would be a great way to help us release the negative energy we had been carrying around with us for way too long. We wouldn't have any regrets after this life, because we would say and do everything that was needed now.

So now I knew *what* to do, but I needed to know *how* to do it. I thought about it and then decided to hold a group meeting. I sent out a mass mailing to all my clients informing them that I was offering a free workshop on the importance of telling our loved ones how much they really mean to us. The turnout for this workshop was so huge that there was standing room only. I even had to turn some people away, because there was no more space.

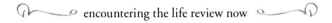

Participants who were serious about doing the practice were asked to write these letters and, if they felt guided to do so, to mail them to the recipients. Then I set another meeting date to see what had transpired. Little did I know how much this simple little exercise was going to literally change the lives of the letter writers—and the recipients as well.

seeing through the eyes of those closest to me

We are all on different journeys and, at times, encounter certain obstacles along the way. Most of us are so wrapped up in our own lives that we are not able to see another's point of view. This can be especially true when we are dealing with those who are the closest to us. When we are having so-called problems with people who are in our lives, a normal response is to only see what they are doing to us. The drawback, however, is that their reaction is the same: they only see how *we* are affecting *them*.

The assignment for participants in my initial letter-writing workshop was to write letters to the people who were most important in their lives. Participants were to write the letters as if they were looking back at their lives with their loved ones, so that they had a broader perspective on what really had happened. In the letter, they were to tell their loved ones just how much they meant to them, what they loved about them, and why they were proud of them. While writing, they also needed to see everything from the other person's point of view. In other words, the writers needed to really try to see just how they had affected the other person, in both good and bad ways.

The bottom line was that the letter should be, for the most part, a positive one—for both the letter writer and the person to whom the letter was written. When acknowledging positive situations, writers were asked to discuss what helpful, loving actions they would continue to perform. When recognizing negative circumstances, writers were told to ask for forgiveness and discuss how they would remedy the situation.

The purpose of this experiment was to create peace in the lives of both the letter writers and the recipients. It took me by surprise, however, when it became the greatest healing experience of my own life!

My Experience with Writing Letters to My Children

I wanted to see firsthand how writing letters to my own loved ones would affect me and the people in my life, because I had just gone through a divorce a year before and was trying hard to keep everything as normal as possible within my family. I knew that the letters to my children and my ex-husband would be the most difficult, yet the most important ones, to write.

I began by writing to my older son, Chris. At the time, he was living in New York City, where his job had taken him. In the letter, I explained that writing to him was a great opportunity to tell him exactly how much he meant to me. I continued by saying how my life had changed for the better when he was born, and I told him how lucky I was to have been a stay-at-home mom with him when he was younger. I talked about all the wonderful things that I remembered about him from when he was growing up, and I went into detail about why I was so proud of him.

I also knew that I had to talk about any events that I regretted. "When you were in the seventh grade, things turned around a little. You became quiet, and I didn't want to interfere. To be honest, I didn't know how to deal with this, because we had been so close before that. I felt that you wanted me to leave you alone, so that's what I did. I shouldn't have done that. I should have hugged you more (because I truly wanted to, but didn't want to bother you) and told you more often how I felt (because I loved you and still do so much). I thought you needed space, but I should have continued to show you affection anyway. We lost that special closeness, because I backed away. I'm so sorry, and I want you to know that I adore you. If I could make up for all those hugs I missed giving you at that time, I would do it all right now!"

I then discussed why I was sorry about the divorce and what I could have done differently. I also went into much more detail in my letter to him about why I loved him so much and made sure to include that he was everything I would ever want in a son—because he is! I knew it was complete when I finished writing the fourth page. Then I signed it and stuffed it into an envelope.

The following night I wrote a letter to my daughter, Jessica. I knew this letter was going to be a tough one to write, because Jessica was away at college when my ex-husband and I were going through the divorce. Although she was seemingly out of the

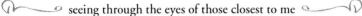

picture when everything happened, it still had negatively affected her in a big way.

Jessica and I had always been very close over the years, and I wanted it to stay that way. I felt so horrible: first, because she was hurting so badly from the divorce and, second, because I felt as if it may have ruined my relationship with my daughter, whom I loved so very much.

So, I began the letter in the same way as I had done with Chris's letter, by explaining why I was writing it. I talked about why I was so proud of her—from the time she was a baby until the present time. I went on to tell her why I was sorry about how the divorce had affected her:

> *If there was another thing I would say "I'm sorry" about, it's the fact that Dad and I didn't get along and how that affected you, Chris, and Tim. Dad and I both tried to make the best of things and make it work—especially for you guys. What it basically comes down to is that he and I are such opposites; no one is bad or wrong. I'm actually going to write a letter to him too, telling him what I need to say. It'll be good stuff—not to worry. I truly want peace in all our lives. Yes, maybe the two of us could have tried harder, but*

sometimes being peaceful means moving on in life so that we can pursue the things we need and love to do. And both of us can do that now.

As you know, I am also trying to keep the peace with Dad's family. They are all sweethearts, and I wouldn't want it any other way. If I don't do it perfectly, please know that I am trying, okay? Maybe I'll make mistakes along the way, but I certainly don't want to hurt anyone in the process.

I only want what is best for all of you, and I'm finally figuring out what's best for me too. It's quite a learning experience, and I do know that everyone is growing from it all.

I didn't want to end the letter with regrets, so I then expressed why I was grateful for certain things and wrote that I knew I was a good mother. I also made sure to let her know what an awesome daughter she was! I thanked her, and told her how much I loved her and why I was so proud of her. When I was finished, I felt as if an enormous weight had been lifted off my shoulders. I printed the letter, signed it, and put it into an envelope.

My next letter would be to my younger son, Tim, who had lived at home during the transition, watching me pack all our belongings and moving with me to our new house. In my letter to him, I mentioned some of the funny things he had done when he was growing up, and why I was so thankful that I had been able to stay at home with him when he was small. I went on to express that I was glad I had been there for all those wonderful moments, and went over all the reasons why I was so proud of him.

Then I knew that I had to deal with my regrets:

When you got older and didn't need me as much as when you were little, I started to work. This new way of life outside of the house was a great experience for me for the most part, but I do regret some things—like missing some Saturday baseball games because I had appointments. (As you know, since I scheduled the appointments so far ahead of time, I couldn't change them, and I regret that so much.) I also miss not being at home with you on certain days when you are off from school. Even though you don't need me in the way that you did when you were younger, I still want to be there for you. Hopefully, you realize that you, Chris, and Jessica will absolutely always come first in my life.

As in Chris's and Jessica's letters, I mentioned how sorry I was about the divorce, and further explained how I was doing everything I could to continue to keep the peace with the entire family.

Then I went on to talk about Tim's going off to college the following year:

> *Tim, soon you'll be off to college and basically on your own, so you won't be here when I come home every day. I'll truly miss you so much. Even though you mostly stay down in the basement while I'm upstairs, I know you are there, and that's so comforting. I know without a doubt that you are going to "make it big" because of your wonderful ability to see and feel the completion of all your goals! I just want you to know how much I really love you for who you are and what you have become.*

I went on to thank him for his amazing qualities and talked about why I was proud of him. Then I ended the letter with:

> *Okay, here are just a few words of wisdom. Please remember to do what you love in life. Don't settle. Make sure you enjoy whatever job you take after college. Yes, making a lot of*

money is good, but please understand that it's even more important to be happy. Also, try to remember to have fun. Create a balance of work and play, and enjoy life!

Finally, know that I am here for you and always will be, and I am so proud to be your mother. Please don't ever change. I love you so much and just wanted you to know that.

Ahh, I had now finished writing the letters to my children! I printed Tim's letter, signed it, and stuffed it into an envelope. Now, I was ready to give the letters to them.

Since my two younger children were living at home, I simply placed the letters on their desks on Valentine's Day. I mailed the one to my older son a few days before February 14 to make sure he'd get it in time. Then I waited.

☺ ☺ ☺

After he read his letter, my younger son, Tim, who, at that time, was a man of few words, came upstairs as I was making dinner and thanked me. He stayed and chatted with me for a while, and I enjoyed that so much.

Later that evening, after my daughter, Jessica, had come home from work and read the letter, she came downstairs to give me a big hug. She told me how much she loved me and appreciated the letter I had written to her. I was so glad she was now able to understand just how much I really cared and wanted to make things better.

I had to e-mail my older son, Chris, a few days later to make sure he had received my letter. He confirmed by e-mail that he had received it, and thanked me very much.

As you can see, each of my children has his or her own personality, and on the surface, it didn't seem that I'd made much progress at all. However, the real effects weren't apparent right away; all of that came about later. We all became closer, and I could feel that the resentment was gone. Chris started coming to visit more often, Jessica began confiding in me again, and Tim was opening up to me as well.

I wondered if I would receive a letter back from them, but I knew it really didn't matter if I did. I was so happy that I had healed my relationship with each of them. However, I was totally surprised at what transpired on my birthday, a month and a half later.

My Birthday Surprise

My children decided to take me out to eat on my birthday. I was so excited to be with all of them on my special day. We dined at my favorite Mexican restaurant and then returned to my house to have cake that Jessica had made. Chris asked if we could wait for his girlfriend, Jamie, to come over before we had the cake, and, of course, I agreed.

When Jamie arrived, Jessica asked me to sit down on the couch, because they had a surprise for me. She took out a DVD that featured pictures of my children and me on the cover. Jessica placed it into the DVD player as I sat waiting in anticipation. I just knew this really was going to be something very special!

The first person who came on the screen was my mother. I was surprised and asked Jessica, "When did you go to Grandma's?" I looked over at her, and she just smiled.

My mother started talking about her memories of when I was younger, and said how much she loved me and why she was proud of me. It was so very touching that I began to cry. Then my sister came on as well. She reminisced about our childhood and said that she loved me.

After that, Jamie came on the screen. She recalled some funny memories from our times together, including when all of us gave my dog Benny a bath in the backyard. She also talked about when she had brought her dog Corky over to see my pool. At that time, my other dog, Chelsea, came outside, too, and because she wasn't paying attention, she fell into the pool. Jamie spoke about how I had jumped into the water to save her, even though I couldn't swim and had a terrible fear of the water. She went on to say that this was a perfect example of the type of thing that she said I do, "thinking of others, even at the risk of your own life." I tried very hard to hold the tears in as I listened to her loving words.

Then Tim appeared on the DVD and talked about a trip to Boston I had taken with him and his friend Sam. He thanked me for always laughing with him and putting up with all the pranks he had pulled on me over the years. He went on to tell me how grateful he was for other things as well, and said that he loved me very much. I wanted to hug him right there, on the spot!

Then Jessica appeared on the screen and said how much she loved me. She told me I was always supportive of her and never judged her. She went on to thank me for helping her to "see the world through loving eyes." You can understand why, at this point, I was totally losing it. I felt so loved and was extremely thankful for what my children had done for me. I knew that Jessica was the mastermind of this project, and I was also aware of just how much time and energy she had spent to make it all happen!

Then Chris came on the screen and spoke about things I couldn't even believe he remembered! He reminded me of how much he had loved dinosaurs in preschool, and mentioned how I had bought him every dinosaur book and toy I could find. I started to laugh, because that was so true. He went on to say how much I had helped him throughout his school years, and talked about some "words of wisdom" I had given him before he had made his valedictory graduation speech in high school. (To make it easier for him to speak in front of everyone, I had told him to imagine everyone in the audience in their underwear.) He then said how proud of me he was for taking my passion in life, creating a thriving business, and becoming an author. Then he ended by saying how much he loved me.

At this point, I thought the DVD was over, but then my pets appeared on the screen too. My dog Benny came on and barked loudly. There was a subtitle underneath him that read, "Mama, there's something I want to tell you."

My other dog Oreo then barked in Benny's face, and the subtitle read, "Look at me! You always get the attention!"

After that, my cat, Mikey, came on the screen looking extremely bored, and the subtitle read, "Oh, those crazy dogs!"

And finally the words, "We love you!" appeared on the screen. (A week after I watched the video, my dog Oreo died, so I am especially thankful that she was on this DVD!)

Now, you would think all this, in itself, was good enough. But then the song "Story of My Life" came on, and the video continued with a series of photographs of some of the most important memories of my life. They started from when I was little and continued until the present time. After my children began to get older in the pictures, a subtitle on the screen read, "And then a few years passed by," and pictures of me signing books and teaching angel classes appeared. At this time, Louis Armstrong's "What a Wonderful World" was playing in the background. I literally had "angel bumps" all over!

Finally, this wonderful DVD ended with the words, "You have accomplished so much . . . ," followed by a pause, and then, ". . . and have so much ahead of you. We are all so proud of you. We love you! Happy Birthday."

I had just received the best present I'd ever received in my life. I couldn't control my tears, so I ran upstairs to wipe off the mascara that was running down my face.

◎ ◎ ◎

My children absolutely were affected by the letters I had written to them. The effects weren't so apparent at first, but I know that the letters changed their relationships with me forever. As for me, once again, I felt as if a weight had been lifted off my shoulders. I knew if I were to leave the earth at that time, I would be truly at peace with myself and with my children, because I had told them everything I needed to say.

Writing those letters to my children was one of the best things I have ever done, not only because it helped me to make amends with them after the divorce, but also because it was a great opportunity for me to tell them just how much they were loved. Yes, they knew how much I loved them before the letters, but now everything was down in writing and could be read over and over again throughout the years.

And, as an added bonus, my children took the same concept and made me a wonderful DVD telling me how much they loved me as well!

The Letter to My Ex-Husband

The next letter that I wrote was to my ex-husband. Many things had been left unsaid during and after our 25-year marriage, and I knew I had to get all of that down on paper. I began to see that our inability to communicate had been one of our pitfalls, and this was a good opportunity to let it all out. Remembering that the letter was to be a positive one, I sat at my computer and began to write. While writing, I realized that the bottom line was that we were complete opposites and that this was why everything ended the way it did. Neither of us was bad. We just wanted different things. I realized that I should have supported him more in his interests and that he should have supported me in mine.

I realized that I was thankful that he had been a good provider, which had enabled me to stay at home to raise our children. I also recognized that when he mostly had been concentrating on work, and I on taking care of the children and house, neither of us really had seen the full value of all that the other did. He eventually did become very successful and the children turned out wonderful, so we both accomplished what we had wanted. The unfortunate thing was that we didn't do what was best for us and didn't become the perfect role models for the children, that of parents who demonstrated their love for one another.

As I was jotting all of this down in the letter, I began to understand that we did the best we could, and the past was over. We are truly both at peace with the present situation, and that is the way it should be.

Although the letter was mostly positive, I did stand up for myself. I wanted to allow him to understand my point of view too; that was important. The bottom line was that we both had gone in different directions. His path was good for him, and my path was good for me; but neither was good for the other.

I ended the letter by wishing him the very best in life and expressing that I wanted him to be happy. I thanked God that we each finally had found the tranquility we needed, and I asked if we could continue to keep the peace between us—for ourselves and for the kids.

And as I ended the letter, I realized that even though it had ended the way it did, we're both good people who deserve to live happy lives. I sent the letter, knowing that it was the right thing to do. Then I waited.

◙ ◙ ◙

The following week, as I was checking e-mails between sessions at work, I noticed one from my exhusband. I just glanced at it, because I knew that I really didn't have time to process the whole thing before my next appointment. All I saw was one word: *skeptical.* At first I thought it was going to be a negative letter, so I closed it for the moment. Because I needed to be in the right frame of mind for my appointment, I signed off the computer and tried to meditate.

After a few minutes, I changed my mind and turned the computer back on to check that e-mail, and I'm so glad I did. It basically said that at first he had been skeptical, thinking that it was a letter from my lawyer, but then he had read it. He thanked me and wrote a very nice e-mail response.

I had written down all that I had needed to say, and he had read it. There were no more words left unspoken, and I hoped that he now understood more about where I was coming from. I felt relieved

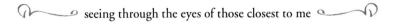
and knew that all was well at that point. The tension between us was finally gone.

Since then, we have e-mailed back and forth about our children and pets, and when we see each other at the children's events and family functions, we communicate more than we ever did before. I feel that we are finally free to move on in our lives—peacefully, with a clear understanding of why everything happened the way it did.

As for me, this whole process also helped to remove the guilt I had been feeling over having a failed marriage. Friends often ask me how I can retain this peace between my ex-husband and his family. I tell them that after 25 years together, it is truly the only way I can get through it all!

letters to other family members

Now it was time for me to write letters to my parents and my sister. In these letters, I knew I needed to write about childhood memories as well as more recent ones. I started with a letter to my mother, because her birthday was coming up shortly and I wanted to place the letter in her birthday card.

The Letter to My Mother

This letter was a very easy one to write, because we had always been close. I started with words that I truly meant:

You are the best mother a daughter could ever have. I always knew you'd be there for me when I was growing up, and I know that you'll always be here for me now.

As an adult, I was now able to see all that my mother had done for me. Unfortunately, I had taken all of that for granted when I was younger:

I didn't understand the extent of all that you had to do to raise me. You worked so hard to support Nora and me, and you never complained. Then you came home and took care of everything that needed to be done at home too. I only wish you would have asked me to help you. As a child, I didn't know any better. Now I do. You shouldn't have done it all yourself.

I wanted to tell her that I now fully saw the bigger picture of being a mom:

I truly didn't understand all that you did, until I got married and had my own kids. I didn't realize all the work that was involved—the cooking, cleaning, shopping, washing, and everything else—in taking care of a household and raising kids. It was truly a full-time job.

Most important, I also had to tell her how much I knew she had cared:

> *I want you to know that I absolutely always felt loved.*

I was aware that I had to add some of my regrets as well, so I added:

> *My only wish is that you lived closer. I work such long hours and then continue to do everything that needs to be done at home. Sound familiar? If you lived closer, we could see each other so much more.*

I ended the letter by telling her how alike the two of us were and wrote:

> *Mom, I learned it all from you. I love you so much, and I'm so proud of you for who you are and what you have done with your life. You are so special to me, and I just wanted you to know that. Happy Birthday, Mom. You are the best!*

On her birthday, I gave my mother her presents and card. Because the letter was four-pages long, she said she would read it after everyone had left. When I arrived home, my mother called me, crying, and thanked me for the letter. I was so glad that I had written down all that I needed to say. Nothing really changed right away, because I had already told my mother throughout the years most of what I had written down. However, it was nice that it was now on paper for her to read whenever she needed to be reminded of just how much I loved her.

◎ ◎ ◎

In January 2011, after the first printing of this book, my mom made her transition to the other side. The day before she passed, she was unaware of what was going on around her. As she lay in bed, I was *so* happy to see the letter I had written to her lying on her desk. It had everything I needed to say, so I pulled up a chair and softly read those words to her. Although she had not responded earlier to anything, as I was reading my letter of love to her, the expression on her face completely changed, and she raised her hands to her mouth. She had *heard* me! What a blessing it was that I had already written down these perfect words and was able to read them to her during her final days. Everything I needed to say was said, and I had no regrets. What a blessing this was for me and for my mom as well!

The Letter to My Sister

Now it was time to write a letter to my sister. This letter was a little more difficult to write, because, for whatever reason, we hadn't really been close to one another. In the letter, I wrote how proud of her I was that she had helped so many people, including the children she taught, and that she had rescued so many animals. Since I had never verbalized this to her, I believed it would be nice to write it all down. I also expressed that I loved her and wanted her to know that I appreciated all that she did.

I never anticipated that my sister would respond the way that she did. She wrote back that instead of making her feel good, it made her feel very sad about our relationship. She stated that I hadn't incorporated anything in the letter about our relationship and the reason was that there wasn't much to tell. She added that she wasn't voicing her thoughts to cause a rift or convey animosity. Rather, it was an attempt to make our relationship better and to heal it over time.

As I read her letter, I felt awful, too. It certainly didn't help that I had opened it right after receiving a telephone call telling me that my friend Marion would probably pass away within the next day or so. To be honest, I was an emotional wreck, and felt numb.

For the moment, I had to push away all that was going on in my life, and I saw that my sister was right. We really didn't have a relationship, and reading her letter made me realize that I needed to do something about it. I called her, not really knowing what to say. After both of us admitted our past mistakes, we arranged to get together for lunch at a distance halfway between us.

We did meet a few days later, and she brought my niece and our mother with her. After that day, we continued to make an effort to meet each other more often, and I'm happy to say that I'm now much closer to my sister than I ever was before. During the last month alone, I have actually seen her five times for a number of different reasons.

Remember, my whole purpose in writing these letters was to go through my life review now, before it was too late, and to heal my relationships; my experience with my sister truly did all that. However, I must be honest about how I felt when I received her response. I truly intended it to be a positive experience, and didn't expect to receive negative feedback. Even though I didn't want to admit it, I was hurt that she took it differently from how I had intended it, and I was mad at myself for taking the time to write to her. On top of it all, this experience came at a very difficult period in my life. However, my sister was absolutely correct, and because of my letter to her, she responded with what was truly needed for our relationship to heal!

I'm very happy that our relationship is so much better, and I am making an effort to show her that I do care and want to be a part of her life. I love my sister, and I am sorry that I hurt her, although it was unintentional. The bottom line is that we are much closer now because of the letter I wrote. I'm truly grateful that we are actually taking the time to show each other that we really do care.

The Letter to My Father

While I was writing the letter to my father, as the rules stated, I needed to see his point of view throughout everything, just as I would see it in my life review. My mother and he had divorced when I was about 15 years old, and for the most part, he'd been out of my life since then. I truly never held a grudge about that, but sadly, I had no relationship with him, other than seeing him at an occasional wedding or funeral every five or six years. I must admit that when I was writing the letter, it was difficult for me to see how I had affected him in a negative way. I did try to call him every so often, and I sent the occasional birthday card in the beginning. Whenever I did pick up the phone to call him, I'd hear that I should call more often; yet he would never call me, so eventually I just stopped trying. However, the point here is not what he should have done; it's what *I* should have done differently.

So, in the letter, I began by writing that, ever since his divorce from my mother, our lives had taken separate paths and that, although neither of us had done it intentionally, it had happened nonetheless. I told him that I knew he'd done the best he could at the time and that I only wished we could have kept our connection in the midst of it all. I did mention that I felt the divorce had been a good thing for him and my mother, because it had enabled both of them to move on from a relationship that really wasn't working out.

Then I remembered that he had been upset when I had my mother—not him—give me away at my wedding so many years ago. I explained why I made that choice in the letter and added:

I actually had told Mommy that I wanted both of you to walk me down the aisle, but she had said it would hurt her very much. I just couldn't cause her pain. I hope you can understand that. That didn't mean I didn't love you. I didn't want to hurt you either, and I'm truly sorry I did.

I knew that I needed to speak up for myself in one area. I mentioned how it was the parents who were the adults when a divorce occurred, and it was the parents' responsibility to reconnect with their children. Having just been through a divorce myself, I saw just how important this was. I also added that everyone reacts differently to stressful situations, and that this was okay too.

I didn't realize, though, the extent to which I had stuffed down many of these emotions for such a long time, believing it was my fault that we weren't close to one another. I now saw, as I was thinking things through while writing this letter, that, in reality, it was not all my fault. We both should have tried more to connect with the other.

I certainly didn't want this letter to be a negative one; that was not the purpose of it at all. I just wanted him to see my point of view, and I wanted to try to see his. The bottom line was that I loved him and wanted him to know that, and I told him so at the end of the letter.

◙ ◙ ◙

Quite some time had passed since I had mailed the letter to my father, and I still hadn't received an answer from him. I began to think he wasn't going to respond. At least I knew I had tried, and it was now in his hands. His response finally came to me in the mail just as I was about to sit down to write about it for this book.

I admit that I was afraid of what he was going to say in response. However, I was so pleased when I began reading it. He began by writing that he was really happy to hear from me, and he discussed how he wished our relationship could have been better. As expected, he did express that he was "deeply saddened, hurt, and angry" when I chose for my mother to give me away at my wedding. He added that he knew he could have been a better person, and asked me to forgive him. He wrote that he wanted me to understand that he'd never meant to cause me pain.

He also stated that he was proud of me for my accomplishments and wished we had communicated better in the past. He ended by telling me that I hold a special place in his heart and always will.

As you can see, the results from my letter to my father were all that I had hoped for. We had finally apologized and forgiven each other after so many years. In writing our letters to each other, we had achieved the peace that we had desperately needed for so long; it was a liberating experience, to say the least. However, I'm happy to say that it didn't end there.

After the letter, my father called me up on my birthday for the first time in several years and conveyed to me many things that I had always needed to hear. I was delighted that he reached out to me in this way, and I told him I'd very much like for us to get to know each other again. Last week, my sister and I met him in Atlantic City, and we had a wonderful time. I am thrilled with our rekindled relationship and fully understand that it really is never too late to make amends. The best part is that we have promised to —and *will*—continue to keep in touch with one another from this point on. We won't be able to change the past, but we certainly can try to make things better *now* and in the future as well.

a letter to someone
who always came last

After telling all those people in my life what I needed to say, I felt relieved. Yet I still hadn't cleared the air with someone I had always put last in my life. This person had always put everyone else in her life ahead of herself, so I didn't think she would mind if I took care of everyone else before her, especially in the writing of these letters.

When I started writing this letter to her, I began to realize just how badly I had treated her all these years. Only as I wrote did I begin to understand that I needed to become more sensitive to *her* feelings and to begin doing that *now*. This person actually needed to be taken care of the most, because she had been neglected for so long. Yet the cause of neglect was not related to anyone outside of herself; the neglect was self-inflicted. I knew so much about her, yet did so little for her. I realized just how unfortunate that was, but it was absolutely going to change now.

I know so much about this person because I have spent every day of my life with her. If you haven't already guessed, the person is me, and I had *finally* come upon the realization that I was just as significant as everyone else in my life. Although people had been telling me this for years, I needed to fully grasp this concept myself.

The Letter to Myself

When I sat down to write my letter, I knew that I first had to understand why I had treated myself in this way. And I needed to be sympathetic in analyzing the situation, just as I had done in my other letters.

I was anxious to get started and began the letter with:

> *Wow! This one is going to be the hardest. How do I tell you how much I love you, when*

I have always put you last in my life? I'm so sorry I haven't given you my attention and have put everyone's needs before your own. Beginning today, I will try to make you feel good in every situation. It is my duty and no one else's to make sure your needs are met.

Tears were running down my face as I wrote these words. I had only begun to fully realize that the person I had treated the worst in my life was *me!* I now needed to begin practicing self-forgiveness and start treating myself with the respect I truly deserved.

With this realization, I continued:

Karen, I am so very proud of you! You are really a good person. You try very hard to see the best in all situations, and always seek to understand the other person's point of view. The only thing I need to say here is that I wish you would see your own point of view and feel how important <u>that</u> is, too.

Ouch! I was beginning to understand everything more clearly now.

I then decided to write about the positive situations I had created in my life:

I am so proud of you for raising three wonderful children. This is one of your greatest accomplishments. Most of your life has been dedicated to raising these warm, caring, and successful children, and you can surely see the outcome of your devotion.

At this point, I was really feeling pleased with who I was. How sad that I had never completely understood it all until I wrote everything down. No words could fully describe how therapeutic this whole process was for me. I continued to write about other things that I appreciated in myself, including how I had started my own successful business and helped so many people, had written my first book, and had always tried to see the good in seemingly bad circumstances.

After discussing these positive aspects I saw in myself, I also knew that I had to write down what I wished I had done differently. The first thing that came to mind was:

Prior to and during the time of your divorce, you were unable to show the children a home in which their parents loved and were good to each other. However, I know you didn't understand the repercussions of all of this at the time, and you certainly didn't do it on purpose.

I wrote about what I should have done differently in my marriage and ended with:

Please see all the good things in your life now—and there are so many of them! Karen, the bottom line is—you did good, girl! I'm so proud of you for who you are, for what you have accomplished, and for what you are continuing to achieve. I thank you and God, the angels, your family, and your loving friends for that!

Then I signed the letter with:

Many hugs and blessings,
Karen

⊡ ⊡ ⊡

I was amazed by how much writing this letter helped me to really analyze different situations that I had never thought about before. To begin with, it enabled me to explore various qualities I never realized I had.

When I finally used the same standards to evaluate myself that I had used for everyone else, I was forced to acknowledge the positive traits I possessed. In the past, if I had seen others with these same characteristics, I would have noticed how kind they were—but surprisingly, I had never been able to see these qualities in myself.

I was also able to see that I desperately needed to honor and stand up for myself, just as I would for someone else. After writing the letter, I remembered times when I hadn't respected my own wishes, and saw how that had hurt me. Now I knew that I needed to catch myself before putting others first at my own expense. With this realization, I promised I would do better, and I understood how important it was to set aside time for *me*. I was *finally* able to see that I was just as important as everyone else.

Writing the letter also helped me to acknowledge my faults and face certain situations in which I had been less than perfect. While I was in the midst of seemingly bad situations, it was difficult to see the total picture. However, now that I was able to look back on everything that had transpired, I was finally able to come to the realization that I had never done anything wrong intentionally. I'd always done the best I could at the time, and I was not a bad person.

I also became conscious of the fact that I'd learned a lot from my mistakes, and I knew I would try hard never to make them again. These so-called mistakes were actually my life's greatest learning

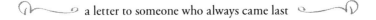

experiences, and I can honestly say I am grateful for all of them.

I can't even begin to put into words how much my life improved after I wrote this letter. Because I'm now able to see everything from a higher perspective, I'm finally able to truly honor myself, and it feels *so* good. I'm now treating myself with the respect I deserve after not doing so for a very long time. Sure, every now and then, I still put the needs of others ahead of my own. Because of this, I make sure to keep my letter handy so that I can reread it whenever I need to be reminded of all that I have learned.

❧ ◙ ☙

a letter to a deceased loved one

Although the purpose of writing the letters I have been discussing is to allow people in our lives to know how much we love them while they are still here on earth, we can also initiate tremendous healing by writing to loved ones who have already made their transition to the other side. Writing this type of letter enables us to get so much off our chests and release a lot of energy that we have been holding on to for so long. I can assure you that, as you are doing this, the recipient of your letter will be able to feel what you are doing, and it will be a wonderful, healing experience for that person as well.

Marion, a good friend of mine, recently made her transition. As she was going through her last hours on Earth, I went to the hospital with the intention of telling her just how much she meant to me. But I arrived at the hospital when members of her immediate family were saying their final good-byes to her, so I turned around and went back home. Although I had missed that opportunity, I knew I could put down on paper everything I needed to say to her, even after she crossed over, and she would still be aware of what I had written.

The Letter to My Deceased Friend

I sat down to write this letter to her when I came home from her funeral a few days later. It was as though she was right there as I was jotting down the words, and it felt wonderful. I incorporated into the letter that I was aware that she was experiencing her life review and that I knew without a doubt that it was a positive one. She was truly experiencing heaven because of all the good she had done in this life.

Marion, how can I put into words just how much you have made the world a better place?

You have always willingly served so many in your path, and I know that you can now see just how much you have helped us all. Doesn't that feel great? I bet you never knew the extent of how much you have affected everyone. It's so sad that you couldn't feel that until now. You have inspired each and every person around you with your love, humor, and concern.

Of course, I also added some of the stories we'd shared, and told her how much I loved her:

Every time we were together, you made me laugh. I always felt so good being in your presence. There are very few people who truly have the special gift you had. Your energy was incredible, and you still made people smile, even when you weren't feeling well.

I can't tell you enough how much I loved you as a human being, and I know you cared for me in the same way. We had an understanding, and we were alike in so many ways. We both put others before ourselves (to a fault!) and did everything for our kids. Neither of us liked to go out; but if someone was in trouble, we'd be there in a second.

We were so different too. For example, you were able to always say whatever was on your mind. I truly wish I could easily voice my opinion like that!

It was such a relief for me to write down all of this. I continued telling her how much I loved her, and ended with:

Okay, Marion, enough with the mushy stuff. You know I love you. Please let me hear from you soon! So many angel hugs, Karen.

Little did I know just how fast she'd come around to let me know that she was aware of the letter I had written to her! That very next weekend, as I was walking down the steps to place letters in my mailbox, a gray bird flew so quickly toward me that I thought she was going to crash right into my chest! She eventually landed on the mailbox and watched me as I stuffed the envelopes inside.

Then she screamed, "Waaaa!" and looked directly into my eyes.

She did it again: "Waaaa!" The bird was desperately trying to get my attention, and I immediately *knew* it was Marion. (Those who have crossed over are able to use their energy to go inside of a bird or any other animal to let us know that they are around us. I will discuss this further in Chapter 11.)

"Marion!" I started to cry. "Marion, oh my God, Marion!"

I had my cell phone in my pocket and immediately called my son, who was in the house, and shouted, "Hurry, come outside. Marion is here!"

He came outside with a puzzled look on his face and then saw the bird still screaming as it was looking directly at me. As I walked up the driveway, the bird continued to follow me.

If my neighbors had heard me, I'm sure they would have thought I had lost my mind! I was answering the bird out loud: "Marion, I love you. I'm so glad you're okay!" After what seemed like an eternity, the bird finally flew away. I went inside, had a good cry, and thanked her for giving me this wonderful gift of letting me know she was okay.

The next day I found out she had appeared as a bird to Carol, a mutual friend of ours. A bird somehow was able to get into the school cafeteria where Carol worked and then started flying all around the room. Carol immediately knew it was our dear friend Marion letting her know that she was there.

Shortly after that, I received an e-mail from Carol relating how another bird had flown into her kitchen and made a *huge* mess all over the walls and floor. Again, Carol was aware that it was Marion, because it was *so* typical of her unique sense of humor.

Needless to say, Carol and I are thrilled that our beloved friend has been giving us signs to let us know that she is around us. There have been countless other times when Marion has made appearances to other family members and friends through messages and dreams, and she still appears as different birds at just the right time.

▣ ▣ ▣

I can't begin to express just how much writing the letter to Marion has helped me. Of course, it certainly made it easier that I really *knew* she was close by and was aware of everything I had written to her. I was able to truly understand on a much deeper level that our friendship didn't just end because her physical body had died. The icing on the cake was when she confirmed her continued existence by appearing to me (and to her other loved ones) a few days after I had requested in the last line of my letter to hear from her soon.

I am so thankful that Marion continues to give us wonderful signs letting us know she is there. It's no surprise to me that Marion is just as feisty as she

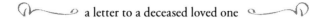

was when she was in her physical body. That is her true essence, and thankfully, that's the way she will *always* be!

❧ ◎ ❧

healing received from the life review

Without a doubt, my life and the lives of those around me have been healed on so many levels because of the letters I took the time to write. I didn't always receive the responses I had anticipated from the recipients of the letters, but the end results were always positive.

Making the Effort to Maintain This Peace with Others

The peace that has come to others and me through my having written these letters is wonderful, but my plan is to maintain this harmony long after the letters have been written. As life goes on, both good and bad issues will arise, and I know I must continue to see things through the eyes of each person I encounter. Although I may not always understand why another person acts in certain ways, I now always attempt to see where that person is coming from. Yes, sometimes it frustrates me when I see that the other person isn't always coming from a place of love, but I try hard not to add any more negative energy to the situation, and it truly helps.

I also know that I can still maintain peace with my loved ones who have made the transition. They absolutely are aware of my words to them and continue to let me know that they are around me. It's so reassuring to know that our love for each other will *always* survive.

Maintaining Peace with Myself

Throughout all of this, I have continued the peace process with myself as well, making sure to remember that I'm just as significant as everyone else. As a result, I can honestly say that I am content with every aspect of my life now.

For so many years, I have willingly and lovingly taken care of my children, and I would never have wanted it any other way. Now that they are grown, it's certainly the perfect time for me to be moving on with my own life. I'm presently seeing a wonderful guy, named Ken, who would do anything for me and treats me as if I were the most important person in the world. We have so much in common, laugh all the time, talk endlessly about anything and everything, and enjoy each other's company so much. He also loves me for who I am, and he encourages me to be all that I can be. Because I feel and act younger than my age, he is a lot younger than I am. In the past, I would have worried about what people thought, but now I know that it really doesn't matter what others feel about the situation; it's about how Ken and I feel. We're doing great, and I can honestly say I've never been happier.

I'm also beginning to do little things during the day to pamper myself. Recently I actually took a day off, which I hadn't done in a long time. I chose to simply relax at home and to write a few words for this book. When I became tired, I put my laptop down and took a much-needed nap. In the past, I would *never* have taken the time to do any of this. As a matter of fact, I can't remember the last time I had a day off before that, even though I have my own business and create my own hours!

Yes, I'm finally treating myself with the respect I truly deserve, and it feels wonderful. Sure, I'm sorry I waited so long to honor myself in this way, but that's okay. What really matters is that I've changed all that, and the time to be happy is *now!*

☉ ☉ ☉

In the next part of the book, I discuss how *you* can go through the same process that I did, and show you how to write these different types of letters to yourself and to your loved ones.

In the following chapter, I cover what I believe is the easier letter to write: the gratitude letter. I will tell you how to write this type of letter and show you the benefits of expressing your love and appreciation to the people in your life.

❈ ☉ ❈

how to experience YOUR OWN life review

the
gratitude letter

An incredibly dedicated group of women had participated in this letter-writing experiment at the same time I did. During our monthly meetings, we discussed how to write the letters, how to overcome any obstacles we encountered, how to deal with any feelings that came up along the way, and, at the later meetings, how the letter writing had affected everyone who was involved. Although a lot of unexpected emotions surfaced during the process, we had a great time, and I can honestly say that we learned so much from each other. Because of everyone's varying needs and expectations, we ended up writing several different types of letters. The first kind of letter we discussed and eventually wrote was the *letter of gratitude*.

Why Write a Gratitude Letter?

Too many of us take for granted the people who are most important in our lives. We know they'll always be there for us, so we don't take the time to let them know just how much we love and appreciate them. Yet those closest to us are often the ones who need to hear our encouraging words the most.

Even if we do verbally tell our loved ones how much they mean to us, sometimes these simple words spoken occasionally don't fully express the extent of our love for them. As part of our experiment, I asked participants in our group—if they felt so guided—to write a letter with words of love and encouragement to the significant people in their lives. All of the results were extremely positive, and some were even life changing. Such was the case with Kathleen, who shares her story so well.

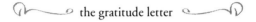

Kathleen's Story

"Several years ago, after my mother passed on, I went through a particularly difficult time in my life for many reasons. I was blessed to have had a wonderfully close relationship with my mother, and we both had supported each other in many ways through the years. She had been an enormous source of emotional strength for me when I was raising my family of five and trying to juggle work and all the other home responsibilities.

"At the time of her passing, I was also going through a very difficult time within my family. I sought the assistance of a wonderful therapist, who helped me begin the healing process. I have always had difficulty communicating my thoughts to certain people in my life, as I have been afraid of hurting their feelings with what I had to say. Thankfully, this has been improving somewhat, but when Karen suggested a project to let our families know the depth of our feelings in the form of a letter, I was thrilled. The plan was to write our most sincere thoughts in letters and deliver them in February, for Valentine's Day. Owing to my large family, it took quite a while for me to write them all.

"I can truly say it was a labor of love and true emotion. Each page was filled with the purest of my thoughts and feelings, particularly for my children. My letter to my husband combined my thoughts of all our positive contributions to our family life with the present state of our marriage and my concern for the future of our relationship. When the letters were complete, I felt as though I had purged my whole being. I cried, laughed, and smiled through them all.

"When I discussed this with my therapist, she calmly looked at me, smiled, and said, 'These letters have done for you in one month what three years of our meetings together couldn't even come close to! I see the look of peace in your face.' She is right.

"My children read their letters with tears in their eyes and have placed them in safe places for the future. One of my daughters has been away at college and didn't feel 'strong enough' yet to read it, as she knows she will want to come home right away.

"My youngest daughter, who is 15, told me she hopes she will be able to read it many times when she is very old. (I found her reading it in bed again the other night after she'd had a bad time with a close friend.)

"For my husband, the letter opened the opportunity for discussion of the status of our lives and

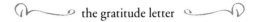

the future. He actually was very moved to read my thoughts and fairly surprised to read the contents of the letter.

"I have since advised several friends of mine to do the same process when they are moved to do it. Karen is right: we often leave things unsaid for too long, and sometimes never get the opportunity in this lifetime to say what we truly feel. For now, I feel very accomplished after this life-altering experience."

☺ ☺ ☺

Kathleen received wonderful results after she wrote everything she needed to say to the people who were most significant in her life. Her family now has a new awareness of her true feelings about them, which has truly helped them all to feel better about themselves and Kathleen as well. Kathleen was finally able to verbalize what she had been keeping inside for way too long. As her therapist said, "The letters did in one month what three years of therapy couldn't even come close to."

Tips for Writing a Gratitude Letter

This type of letter is very easy to write, because it is totally positive. Remember that the purpose of this letter is to make the recipient feel good. You may want to incorporate some or all of your answers to the following questions when you are writing your gratitude letter:

- How does this person make a difference in your life?

- What are some of the things you love or admire about this person?

- Why are you thankful that this person is in your life?

- What are the greatest qualities this person has?

- What are some past events that show the type of person he or she is?

- How do you feel when you are with this person?

- How has this person grown or changed for the better?

- Why are you proud of this person?

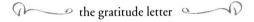

The list can go on and on. The whole idea is to let your loved ones know how you love and appreciate them and how your life is better because they are in it.

You may write this type of letter at any time— for a special occasion or holiday, or just because you want to let the recipients know how much they mean to you. I assure you that the letter will have a profound positive impact on the recipient, especially if it comes at a time when this person needs it the most. This is exactly what happened to me when I received some unexpected letters of gratitude after the experiment ended!

My Unexpected Letters of Gratitude

I received the first letter when a very special woman from our group offered me her beautiful, handwritten words at our last meeting together. In the letter, she explained how the letter-writing experience had given her "a profound feeling of peace." I was so thankful that she had taken the time to do this for me, and this further showed that all that we had been doing the last few months had really made a difference in her life.

A couple of days later, I received an e-mail from another woman in the group, expressing that she had "finally been able to let go of her past and renew her spirit." Then I received more e-mails and letters on consecutive days. One explained, "Now I have a better understanding of why I am who I am." Yet another stated, "Because of your guidance and kindness through this whole process, I am finally at peace."

As I was reading these loving statements, I realized that the group members had written the same type of letters we had been discussing over the last few months. I was truly grateful for these written words, especially because they had come at a time when I needed them most. You see, when I received these letters, I had been working seven days almost every week and was at the point of exhaustion. I was contemplating throwing in the towel at work because I felt so drained, and to be honest, I wasn't even sure if it was all worth it.

Receiving these letters also prompted me to go back to the e-mails I had saved over the past months and years from clients telling me how much I had changed their lives. It took me a while to find these letters, but when I did, I was ever so grateful. Little had I known how these beautiful words of

encouragement were going to help me see that all the hours I had been spending at work hadn't been in vain.

Tears poured down my face as I read what one woman had written: "You have no idea how much of my saddened faith—that I thought I'd lost—you repaired." She went on to say, "You saved me, really. I am deeply, profoundly grateful."

Another woman wrote, "I wanted to thank you once again for everything you've done for us. Your reading has brought me a sense of comfort, understanding—and most important—peace that I didn't think I could feel after all that has happened to us. My world has completely changed for the better. You've done for me what no doctor, psychiatrist, or medication could ever do for me. You've renewed my hope and faith in the Lord and his angels. What you do can't be easy, but I just wanted to remind you that we truly appreciate it."

As I was flipping through the letters, fighting back the tears, I read, "Words can't express what a wonderful feeling it is to know that we are not alone and that we are loved so dearly by God and the angels. I am so grateful to have met someone as special as you. You probably don't realize what a difference you have made in the lives of so many people."

I went on to read another letter: "I just wanted to say thank you so much. My mom has always told me that if everyone in the world lit a candle, what a bright world it would be. Your light is a lighthouse! I just want you to know how nice it is to be around you. Your love is very infectious. In thanks, I have lit a candle for you and your angels for a bit of extra love."

And then I came upon an e-mail that summed up what I really needed to hear at that time: "I just have to write you to let you know that you have changed my life. I have had an amazing growth of renewed faith and a very new relationship with the angels. Karen, you and your work have made a real difference in my life. I am eternally grateful to you."

The encouraging words I received from these e-mails and the many other letters truly renewed my passion for my work so that I was able to continue with what I believe is my true mission in life: to serve and be an instrument of peace to others. I can't begin to explain how grateful I am that the writers took the time to let me know how much I had helped them. The funny thing is, they have no idea how much of a difference they have made in *my* life, so I am writing it down here to tell them how much I truly appreciate *their* encouraging, loving words.

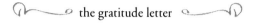
They have literally given me the incentive to continue my work so that I may go on to help those in my path.

The Benefits of Writing a Gratitude Letter

Wouldn't you love to hear that you have made a difference in someone's life? I know you would! Now, try to understand how you can brighten someone else's day by doing this exercise.

If you give your significant loved ones or people who have made a positive impact on your life this type of letter, they will see just how much they are truly appreciated and loved by you. The best part is that they will be able to reread your letters later, enabling them to receive the benefits of your letters long after you have written them.

Who knows? You may even receive a letter of appreciation back from your loved ones, letting you know how much you have made a difference in their lives as well! Now *that* would truly be awesome!

◙ ◙ ◙

In the next chapter, I will talk about a letter that is a little more difficult to write: the forgiveness letter. I will show you how to write this type of letter,

and explain the benefits of writing it when either you need to forgive someone else or you want someone to forgive you.

❧ ◉ ☙

the forgiveness letter

As I gathered thoughts to begin this chapter, I gazed upon a quote from Saint Francis of Assisi that I have painted on my wall: "Lord, make me an instrument of your peace." Just by reading and *feeling* these words within me, I experience the greatest sense of peace.

If you go through life extending love to all of the people you meet, you, in turn, will experience tranquility in your own life. This is because whatever energy you give out, you truly get back—whether now or at a later time.

God's positive, loving energy is within every one of us. When this energy is at the purest level, you are concerned with serving and helping others. It is in being of service to others that you receive whatever you need. In other words, whatever you give to others, you receive back. This is *always* the case.

It is important to see the viewpoint of others and really listen to them. If others feel heard, they don't have to fight against anything, and that's how real peace begins. I once heard Deepak Chopra say that "When you let down all your defenses, there is nothing to attack."

As I stated earlier, in the afterlife you will feel how you have affected others through your actions during your life here on earth. At that point, you will, once again, become conscious of who you really are, without the ego or bodily attachments— connected to everyone and everything.

Of course, you don't have to wait until after you die to feel how you have affected others. The peace within you now is a clear indication of how you are vibrating in this life and of how you are treating others and yourself. If you are not experiencing harmony, look within to see if there is someone you need to forgive or if you need to be forgiven by someone you may have hurt. Remember, true peace doesn't

come from focusing on problems you have with others; rather, it comes from focusing on *solutions* to these problems. If you truly are able to see the other person's point of view, you will then be able to begin the healing process and take any steps necessary to resolve the conflict. A great way to start this process is by writing it all down in a forgiveness letter.

Why Write a Forgiveness Letter?

Telling your loved ones how much they mean to you can be an easy thing to do if you are expressing your love and appreciation to them. A much more difficult letter to write is one in which you seek forgiveness. However, this form of letter is truly the one that will be most beneficial to both you and the person to whom you are writing, and it should help you to release a lot of the negative energy you have been holding on to for so long.

If the type of letter you are writing is one in which you are attempting to forgive someone else, seeing the other person's point of view is crucial. As Einstein once stated, "A problem can never be solved with the same energy that started it."

Staying angry not only hurts the other person, but also hurts *you*. If you cultivate seeds of love, the weeds of hatred will simply wither away.

A letter of forgiveness is also beneficial if you are the one who needs to be forgiven. True healing comes when you are able to see your part, as well as the other person's part, in every situation. When others feel that they are truly being understood, they most likely will begin to try to understand *you* more as well.

Writing a Letter to Forgive Another

When you begin a forgiveness letter, please be sure to include anything you love or appreciate about the person. (See the previous chapter.) This will enable the recipient to see that you are coming from a place of love. Also, always remember not to attack. If your recipients feel harassed, they won't be open to understanding your point of view. When you are writing down the words, think of how you would feel if you were the other person. Recipients of your letters will be responsive only if they feel safe and not judged.

As Neale Donald Walsch says, "You may speak your truth, but soothe your words with peace. Tell your truth gently, kindly, and with compassion for the hearer. Seek to say what needs to be said with softness, and with a wide-open heart."

Writing in this way will make a world of difference, both to you and to the recipient of your letter. You may not always agree with what this person did, but at least you will begin to understand the situation from a broader perspective. Remember that inner peace won't come from a change in circumstances; it will come from a change in your *perception* of the current circumstances.

Finally, conclude forgiveness letters on a positive note so that after the recipients finish reading them, they will continue to experience uplifting feelings from your words. This lasting impression may be the most significant aspect of the whole exercise.

After you have finished writing a forgiveness letter, you may decide whether or not you will mail it to the person. If you don't want to send the letter, don't! Always trust your gut feelings. At least you will be able to release your negative attachments from what happened, and on an energetic level, the other person should *feel* what you have written. On the other hand, if you decide to send the letter, the recipient will see that you are attempting to remedy the situation, and this should be most beneficial to both of you.

Writing a Forgiveness Letter to Be Forgiven

When you write a letter asking to be forgiven, start it off as a letter of gratitude. (See the previous chapter.) After stating how much you love and appreciate the other person, you may discuss why you are sorry for what you did. However, please be kind to yourself and give details from your point of view about why you did these things, so that the other person will be able to understand the situation better. Tell the recipient that you never meant to hurt him or her. Then explain why you wish you could take it all back and why you are sorry.

Remember not to end the letter in a negative tone. Again, tell the person to whom you are writing how much you love him or her, and add some more encouraging statements as well. If your closing remarks are positive, it will give the reader a lasting, peaceful impression.

After you have finished, as stated previously, look within yourself to decide whether or not to mail the letter to the recipient. For this type of letter, you truly

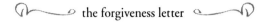

will receive the most favorable outcome if you allow the other person to read what you have written.

After you've written the letter, you should feel empowered and at peace. With this newfound freedom, you may even experience positive changes in your life, including more courage and an increased sense of oneness with others. A high-school teacher from New Jersey experienced this wonderful transformation after writing a forgiveness letter to her brother. The purpose of her letter was twofold: she wanted to let her brother know that she had forgiven him, and she wanted to be forgiven by him as well.

High-School Teacher Finds Peace with Her Brother

One of my favorite clients, Caroline, had stuffed down an assortment of emotions for way too long. The following are her own words describing how the letter-writing experience not only helped her to heal her relationship with her brother, but also allowed her to become a stronger and more assertive person.

"Raised as the oldest child, I was always reminded that I was responsible for my brother and sister. Whenever they messed up, it was my fault, and it was my job to protect them. I wrote my first letter of forgiveness to my sister after I moved away from the family home. Thirty years later, I wrote a long-overdue letter to my brother. I have lived with this guilt for far too long.

"Writing the letter brought mostly stressful memories and emotional tears, but also warm, heartfelt remembrances of good times past. I am still amazed that I actually wrote and sent the letter. This was the beginning of my becoming more assertive. There is a new understanding between my brother and me. We experienced a difficult childhood and survived.

"For nearly 15 years, I'd had very little contact with my brother. When he had left home for good, I had been able to get his phone number through the phone company. The contact my brother and I had was very minimal. Basically, I'd just been making sure that he was alive, and I let him know that he had a family if he needed us. He had never contacted my parents or visited the family home until several weeks before our mom passed. He had never again seen our father.

"After both our parents died, I had reached out by inviting my brother to family holidays. It had taken some time, but he eventually started to come to my house on Thanksgiving and Christmas. He had said very little and it had always been very uncomfortable, but I had been happy that there was at least some contact. He had never opened up about himself, and all conversation had always been awkward. This had gone on for about ten years.

"After I sent the forgiveness letter to my brother, he responded by e-mail. Since that connection, things have been much more comfortable. My brother has called several times this past year just to say hello and see how everything was going. He seems much more comfortable when we are together. He has talked more about his work and asked questions about my kids.

"This past Valentine's Day, he called me and said that if anyone deserved a Valentine, it would be me. He told me this three times in our short conversation! I know that this was his way of saying he loves me.

"He actually sent me an e-mail today telling me what a nice time he'd had on Easter with me and my family. He said I looked very happy and content with life. I told him that I have been working on finding inner peace and possibly we could talk about it someday soon.

"When we met as a group to discuss our letter writing, I was so surprised that I was able to share my experience. Understand that this new self-assertiveness amazed me. I have never been able to speak in front of my peers. This new strength within me is in all aspects of my life. The warmth and love I felt with these women has given me the confidence to express myself. By expressing myself, I know that I am on the road to healing."

◎ ◎ ◎

I have seen firsthand what a wonderful change has come over Caroline since she wrote the letter to her brother. It is incredible how much more confident and at peace she is with herself and others!

The best part was her brother's positive response to her words. A big part of her success was due to the way she had written her letter. The whole tone was extremely gentle and encouraging; she saw the events from her childhood from *his* point of view; she took responsibility and asked to be forgiven for what she had done; and she used encouraging, positive words. Here are just some of the many beautiful words she conveyed to her brother:

I am so glad that the time we have spent together lately has opened up my heart in many ways. It saddens me that I allowed so much time to elapse before I reached out to you. We endured similar experiences during our childhood, but

neither of us took the time to understand how these experiences were affecting the other. Please accept my sincere apologies for not being there for you. I was aware that so many things were happening, but we never discussed them.

She ended her letter with:

I am writing this to tell you I love you. I am proud of who you have become. You are a good person with a caring heart. Please forgive me for any past hurts or lack of support on my part. We are in this life together, and now each day is a new beginning. I am glad you are my brother, and I am here for you with open arms and heart.

Because Caroline was able to write down her feelings to her brother in a letter and build up enough courage to mail it to him, she was able to connect with him on a much deeper level, and their relationship is better than ever. Her brother now feels that he is understood and loved by her, and he wants very much to be in her life again. Her written words created a newfound peace between them—something that they both had desperately needed for so many years.

Through the process of writing the letter, Caroline was able to release feelings that she had stuffed inside for way too long. As an added bonus to this whole experience, she emerged much more self-assured than she had ever been. Thank goodness, she finally sees herself as the person she has always been—a beautiful, loving, powerful woman—and I am honored to have gone through this entire healing experience with her!

When Forgiving Is Difficult to Do

There may be times when forgiving someone may seem almost impossible because you have been hurt so badly. It is during these times when it would be extremely beneficial to you to truly analyze the situation through the other person's perspective. Only after perceiving the circumstances from the other person's viewpoint will you be able to start to understand why that person did certain things; this should then activate a wonderful healing within yourself. Such was the case with Donna, whose mother had been abusive to her throughout her life.

Donna had spent her whole life trying to get her mother's approval and love, but had never received it. Over the years, she was physically and emotionally abused many times, causing her to feel that she was unlovable. Sometimes her mother's verbal abuse was even harder to endure than the physical abuse. Worse yet were the times when her mother had ignored situations in which others mentally and physically abused Donna.

As a young child, Donna would say the rosary every day and ask God to allow her to die so that she wouldn't have to deal with her mother's wrath anymore; her pain was *that* unbearable.

Throughout the years, Donna sought every means possible to heal, whether through therapy, workshops, books, or anything else she could think of to help free her from past wounds. Some of these methods required her to do meditations to heal her inner child, but she couldn't even bring herself to peacefully visualize her mother during these times.

After attending a few of our letter-writing meetings, Donna decided to write a forgiveness letter to her mother, who had died a few years earlier. To say the least, it was extremely difficult for her, but eventually she was able to do it.

According to Donna, "Seeing everything through my mother's eyes helped me to understand things through a different perspective. I finally realized that my mother's problems began because of her own dysfunction. I was able to see that she didn't treat me the way she did because I wasn't good enough, and it wasn't about what she did to me anymore."

After Donna wrote her letter, she was actually able to perform the inner-child, guided meditations that she had attempted so many times before—without "freaking out," as she put it. She was finally able to see that her mother had problems from her own past, stemming from being the youngest of nine children. With this realization, Donna began to see why her mother had not been capable of true nurturing.

Donna further explained, "Therapists make you think about your feelings, but not the feelings of the person who has hurt you. They don't explain why abusers did what they did. I now have a better understanding of why she wasn't a loving mother; she couldn't be—because she didn't receive love herself."

Donna further realized that she had "married" her mother when she was with her first husband, who had also mentally and physically hurt her. Many times, victims of abuse continue to be in abusive relationships until they resolve their inner issues. Thankfully, even before the letter-writing experience, Donna met a wonderful, loving man who adores her and her family, and who treats her with the respect that she has always craved.

I must also add that victims can either carry out the same abuse in their own lives, or they can learn from it. Because I have met her beautiful family, I know firsthand that Donna has learned so much from her childhood about what *not* to do. She is totally devoted to her husband, children, and grandchildren—and it has definitely paid off. Her family adores her, and rightfully so; they are the loves of her life!

The Benefits of Writing a Forgiveness Letter

You will be healed on many levels when you forgive the people in your life. Writing a forgiveness letter with the intention of seeing everything through the other person's eyes is the perfect way to begin. First, ask yourself if you had a role in whatever happened and if you could have done anything differently. Then try to see the full picture of what was going on with the other person as well.

For those times when you feel that you didn't contribute to the negativity at all, try to look at what was going on in the other person's life. You may even need to look farther back to see what occurred in the person's childhood. This should help you to understand that person's negative actions from a higher perspective. As Neale Donald Walsch so perfectly states in his book *The Storm Before the Calm,* "No one does anything inappropriate, given their model of the world."

Please understand that I'm not saying to condone the actions of others who have hurt you. I am saying to forgive the *person,* because as the great Master Jesus said, "Forgive them, for they know not what they do." When you truly understand this concept, miracles will occur in your life, and you will feel like a new person.

In reality, *not* forgiving someone hurts *you* so much more than it hurts the other person. Don't let negative emotions poison your life. From this point on, create your world with love and understanding. Shift your focus from anger and judgment to joy and encouragement. Release the negativity of the past and allow only light to shine in your present. You will see: after you have written your letter of forgiveness and have really let go of past grievances, you will truly be on the road to a much brighter, happier future!

In the next chapter, I will discuss how to write what I believe may be the most important type of letter of all: a letter to yourself. I will also explain just how essential it is to continue to love and respect yourself long after you have written these words down on paper.

the
letter to yourself

Writing letters to ourselves is perhaps the most difficult, yet the most beneficial of all. We tend to direct our focus from the inside looking *out* at others rather than from the outside looking *in* at ourselves. When we do focus on ourselves, too often we notice the negative instead of the positive qualities we have.

How Writing a Letter to Yourself Works

If we were able to perceive our lives from a loving, nonjudgmental outsider's point of view, we would have a broader understanding of our lives so far. The purpose of writing this type of letter is to do just that; with this newfound insight, we'll be able to come to terms with why we did certain things and decide what changes we may wish to make for the future. Even more important, we will begin to see ourselves the way God sees us—as the exceptional, lovable, and magnificent beings that we truly are.

This is exactly what happened to Linda after she wrote a letter to herself. She speaks of this experience as "receiving a wonderful healing and a peaceful response to [her] prayers."

She says, "Writing a letter to myself was perhaps the greatest healing tool I have experienced. I closed my eyes and prayed that God, my guardian angel, and the archangels would be with me to help me write my letter. What happened next was surreal. I began to write from the beginning of my childhood, seeing myself as that sweet little girl with pigtails. The writing was quick and effortless. I felt the words being dictated to me by another source. When I finished, I was left with three pages that held a beautiful message, letting me know how special I was and that it was time to forgive myself once and for all. This really set me free.

"I put down my pen and felt a big release, along with a warm ocean of peace and calmness. Ever since that evening, I have felt at peace. I am grateful for what I was able to receive: an answer to my prayers!"

Linda has been through so much, yet she still has a very positive outlook on life. As stated previously, it took no effort for her to write the letter to herself, and it was most beneficial. She obtained the peace that she had sought, and was very thankful for the outcome.

⊡ ⊡ ⊡

For others, the writing of these letters was more challenging because of various painful memories. However, in the end, it was all worthwhile. Such was the case with Carol, who had a more difficult time looking back at certain events in her past.

"When I began the letter to myself, thoughts just started to rush through my mind. Painful memories kept playing in my head. My pen couldn't keep up with the flow of life's incidents. It was like a life review, starting from yesterday and going back in time until I saw a happy, joyful four-year-old girl in all her pure glory. I took a deep breath and realized that I was filled with so much joy and enthusiasm for life. That is where I now choose to be!

"I tried for days to write down the things I loved about myself, but this was such a frustrating task that I had to stop. I wanted those feel-good moments from when I saw myself as a beautiful child. During the course of the next six weeks, these stressful memories would resurface while I was driving, trying to sleep, or anytime I wasn't actively involved in something. Instead of getting depressed and dwelling on these emotions, I told myself that I had already forgiven everyone involved, including myself, and made a motion as if to throw them out over my left shoulder, never to return. These memories continued to flood my mind. Each time, I reminded myself that I had already forgiven myself and everyone involved. The thoughts come less often now and are not as intense; it's really working!

"My ego now knows that I am releasing all negativity and allowing all the beauty, joy, and spirit to fill me. I have always known that these positive attributes were within me, but I wasn't allowing myself to receive them. I am so proud of myself, because I am headed in the right direction; I will continue to live a life of gratitude and to bring joy to others. I feel so blessed. Within my soul is a smiley face!

"I have always been an extremely active person, and I never had time to think or rest. I was afraid of where my thoughts would lead me. Now I know the stillness that allows me to hear and be at one with spirit.

"Days before our last class, I wrote what I loved about myself. I easily scripted three paragraphs filled with joy, love, and euphoric bliss. It was beautifully written with sincere, heartfelt emotion. Did I write this? Yes!

"Have I beaten away my hurtful past? Not completely, but I am at a better place, where peace is achievable. I now know how to get rid of the negative thoughts and replace them with optimism, love, and hope. I can truly say that I love myself. How lucky I am to be embarking on a new chapter of my life at age 51. This experience has allowed me an opportunity to be without fear, and to open myself up to love and new experiences."

Even though the process wasn't easy, when she had finished writing her letter, Carol obtained a wonderful healing in her life. She was so pleased with her results that she decided to spread her new-found knowledge and peace by incorporating the letter-writing experience into her classroom.

She explains, "I wanted to share my new zest for life with others. Since I am always trying to connect with my students in a way that touches their souls, I decided to take this letter concept to my health classes. I want my students to believe in themselves and to know that they can live their passions and strive for happiness.

"To make it easier for the 16- to 17-year-old students, I composed eight soul-searching questions. I asked them in such a way that the students were able to realize the good qualities that they possessed and to understand how they could transfer them into their life passions and career choices. Many students were amazed at how others saw them and were proud of who they were and what they could accomplish. Many actually expressed how the love of family and friends had given them the strength to live and persevere in an environment of hatred and hardship.

"I was so happy that we were able to break through surface thoughts and reach down to deep, meaningful emotions. I will continue to use this concept to help others find the love and joy in themselves and to spread that miracle on to others."

Carol has been an instrument of peace and is very excited to share her newfound knowledge with others. Throughout this whole process, she has been able to let go of negativity from her past by forgiving herself and the people who have hurt her.

She went on to say, "Over the course of the last few months, I have been able to forgive others and

myself for painful past experiences. I have learned how to replace negative thoughts with optimism and joy. I am grateful for all my gifts, and I know that I am truly blessed. I believe that I can inspire others to see the beauty within themselves so that they can live joyous and passionate lives. I am on my true path in life. *Miracles* await me!"

Tips on Writing a Letter to Yourself

Okay, now it's time for you to write your letter to yourself. Remember, the purpose of this letter is for you to feel better; its tone should always be positive, loving, and encouraging.

The following are some guidelines you may use. You don't have to include everything listed here, but it would be most beneficial to you if you did.

- Write as if you were speaking to someone else.

- Discuss why you love yourself.

- Mention your proudest accomplishments and your best qualities.

- Write about what you can do differently to make yourself feel better.

- If you are unhappy with certain things you have done, state that you forgive yourself; look at the events with a new understanding of *why* you did what you did.

- Make sure to conclude the letter with loving, positive statements.

The Benefits of Writing a Letter to Yourself

With the other types of letters, you were focusing on seeing everyone else's point of view. Of course, while it's important to treat others with respect, you should always love and value yourself as well. If you serve others to the point of exhaustion, you are not giving yourself the love you need, and you will resent giving away all of your energy. You are no less important than anyone else; as a matter of fact, if you put yourself first, then you are in a better position to help and serve others.

As I stated before, although writing a letter to yourself may be the hardest one to write, it will also be the most therapeutic. When you observe yourself from a higher perspective, it will be easier for you to notice more of your positive qualities and discover what changes you can make to improve your life. You'll also be able to genuinely realize that you did the best you could, given the circumstances of your life.

Another great benefit of this type of letter is that it should cause you to become more self-assured. After writing her letter, Kathy, from our letter-writing group, said, "I feel that I've gotten my self-respect back." Another group member, Lauren, stated, "That letter really freed me. I have a greater sense of self-worth, and I now have higher expectations of myself and others."

When you come to the full realization of your importance, your whole life will change for the better. However, remember that it's an ongoing process, and you should continue to honor yourself long after you have written your letter.

After You Have Finished Writing the Letter to Yourself

After writing the letter to yourself, you will see what you need to accomplish to make your life more pleasurable. Use this newfound knowledge to do whatever is needed to make this possible. Don't rely on someone else for happiness; take the necessary steps to make *yourself* happy.

Upon waking in the morning, look in the mirror and say, "I love you! I promise to make you happy today. What can I do to make you feel good?" Then, really listen to yourself and honor your intentions. Don't put things off because you are the last person on the totem pole. Putting yourself *first* will enable you to be there for everyone else.

Finally, because life may take you in many different directions, you may want to write yourself another letter every now and then to reinforce what you've learned from your original letter. In these later letters, you may just want to add on to whatever you've already written, or you may even want to start from scratch. In any case, you will always be reminded of just how much you love, honor, and are proud of the amazing person that you truly are—whenever you decide to revisit your own special words!

◉ ◉ ◉

In the next chapter, I discuss how to write letters to your deceased loved ones, and explain why writing these letters can be very healing—both to you and to those who have crossed over!

❦ ◉ ❧

writing to those who have passed

What happens if you want to say certain things to your loved ones after they have already crossed over to the other side? Is it too late for you to let them know what you are feeling? The answer is no, it's not too late. Writing a letter to a deceased loved one would actually allow you to get the right words out to that person so that you can feel better on many levels.

Of course, there may be a number of reasons why you would want to write to your departed loved ones. The first reason would be to try to come to terms with certain problems you had with them when they were still here.

Unresolved Issues

Maybe you had unresolved issues with your deceased loved ones before they died, and have been holding on to that resentment, guilt, or shame. Writing letters to them will enable you to release a lot of the stagnant energy you have stored inside yourself for way too long.

A young woman, named Amy, had been working on her relationship issues with her boyfriend for quite some time while he was still here on earth. Little did she know that her phone conversation with him one evening was going to be the last one they ever had.

"I was on the phone with my boyfriend, Chris, one night while he was walking home. The next thing I knew, someone had shot and killed him. It was fast and absolutely unbelievable. I didn't know what to think, do, or believe. We had been arguing more than usual, and then, in the middle of our working on our relationship, he was dead. After he died, I wasn't focused on the relationship. I was still reeling from the fact that he had passed away.

"Two years later, I started to write him letters, not just my usual "I miss you" letters, but letters dealing with our relationship. I felt that I still had issues that I needed to work out, and if he wasn't here physically, I was still going to work out my emotions. I really got into my feelings. I wrote letters as if he were sitting in front of me. A lot of crying and anger needed to be released.

"When he passed away, I never focused on our problems—just the fact that he was gone. I felt guilty about being angry at him, so I was in a constant state of grieving. Writing the letters to him gave me the chance I never had to speak to him about us. I released all my anger and frustration.

"After about a month, I met someone, and I have been with this person for a little over a year. I know in my heart that writing the letters to Chris allowed me to clear my mind and heart. Then the Universe was able to deliver to me someone who was loving and kind."

⊡ ⊡ ⊡

At first, Amy needed to recuperate from the trauma of losing her boyfriend in such a horrible way. A few years later, she realized that she also needed to come to terms with many unresolved issues in their relationship. Because Amy was totally numb, she had disregarded these matters for quite some time. She was finally able to move forward after she expressed herself in letters to her deceased boyfriend. At this point she was able to attract what she had always desired in life: a positive, loving, healthy relationship with a man who adored her.

Continued Correspondence with People Who Have Passed

Writing to your deceased loved ones is also an ideal way to keep your connection alive with them. You can obtain so much peace by jotting down your feelings to them and knowing that they truly are around and able to see what you have written.

Ryan, a sweet 12-year-old girl who had recently lost her beloved mother after a long illness, found comfort in doing just that. Lori, her mom, came through during a class I was teaching on how to communicate with deceased loved ones. Lori's message to her precious daughter was to "keep writing" to her. Ryan tells her story perfectly.

"Writing to my mom is the only thing I can do to know that she is still here. I really can't do anything about her dying, but she can still show me signs. Some people might think it's crazy that I write to my mom, but I know she can see it. Even though she's not physically with me doesn't mean that she isn't right here beside me, seeing everything I'm going through.

"For me, writing is the best way to communicate with her—unless it's through Karen—because if I talk out loud to my mom during class, people will begin to think I'm a psycho. During a class, my mom wouldn't leave Karen's side until she'd told my dad that she saw me writing to her, and to write as much as possible. She wanted me to know that she is really watching over me, even though I can't see or feel her.

"Mommy, I know you can see this now. Just know that I love you and miss you.

"What I am about to write probably goes for everyone who has crossed over. As my mom said, 'Remember me how I lived, not how I died.'"

◎ ◎ ◎

How wonderful it is that Ryan instinctively knew that she should write to her mom on a regular basis! Her loving mother, Lori, confirmed that she was aware of what Ryan had written to her, when she came through with a message for her daughter when we all least expected it—right in the middle of a class I was teaching—to acknowledge that very fact.

Tips for Writing a Letter to a Deceased Loved One

You may use many of the guidelines from the previous chapters, with minor modifications, when writing letters to your deceased loved ones. However, just because they aren't physically here to respond to you, rest assured that they will still be aware of what you have written. The most important thing to remember is that they can fully understand what you are feeling, because they are now able to see things from a much higher perspective.

A Letter of Appreciation

Here are just some of the questions you may want to cover in your letter. Of course, you don't have to answer all of them, but it would be most beneficial if you did.

- How did this person make a difference in your life?

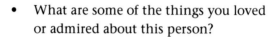

- What are some of the things you loved or admired about this person?

- Why are you thankful that this person was in your life?

- What are the greatest qualities this person had?

- What past events show the type of person he or she was?

- How did you feel when you were with this person?

- How did this person grow or change for the better during his or her life?

- Why were you proud of this person?

A Letter of Forgiveness

Dealing with the grief of losing your loved one is difficult in itself, but even more so when you didn't have the perfect relationship with that person. Writing a letter of forgiveness is an effective way for you to release negative energy that you may have been holding inside for a long time. Here are some guidelines to help you.

When you are forgiving this person:

- Be sure to include anything you loved or appreciated about the person.

- Try to understand what the person did from a broader perspective. In other words, see it from that person's point of view. (When you are really able to accomplish this, you should experience a newfound inner peace. Understand that this peace doesn't come from a change in what happened, but from a change in your *perception* of what happened.)

When you want the person to forgive you:

- Start off the letter as a note of gratitude. After you state how much you appreciate the other person, express that you are sorry for what you have done.

- Be kind to yourself and give details from your point of view as to *why* you acted in a certain way.

- At the end, add any other positive statements you wish to include, and tell the person to whom you are writing how much you loved him or her.

A Letter to Maintain Your Connection

You may just wish to let loved ones know what you are doing and that you are thinking of them. For this type of letter, simply write down whatever you want to say, as often as you feel guided to do so.

What to Do with the Letters after Writing Them

After you have finished writing your letters, you may put them in a place that is meaningful to you. This will give you the security of knowing that you can reread the letters anytime you choose.

You may even wish to hold a special ceremony, such as burning the letters, as a symbol of releasing your words as they are delivered to your loved ones. This is exactly what Marti did after she wrote to her beloved father who had passed away so many years ago.

"Writing is a good way to tell a departed loved one all the things we could never say, so I wrote a letter to my father. It helped me tremendously and brought me peace after all these years. I wrote how I loved him and was sorry that he didn't see us all as we grew up. He was a gardener, and roses were his specialty, so I decided to plant some roses on my balcony. After I burned the letter out in the garden, I buried the ashes in the rose pots."

◎ ◎ ◎

By writing a letter to her father, Marti was able to obtain the closure that she had sought for many years. She was able to incorporate her letter writing into a ceremony in which she symbolically joined her words with the very soil in which her father's favorite flowers grew.

The Benefits of Writing a Letter to a Deceased Loved One

Of course, it's best to tell your loved ones whatever you want them to know while they are still here in the physical body. However, it's not too late to do so after they have already crossed over to the other side; you will still be able to receive tremendous satisfaction by expressing your feelings to them. Writing letters also gives you the perfect opportunity to say everything you need to say to those loved ones who were never able to listen to you when they were physically here. Whatever your objective is—to forgive, to be forgiven, or just to keep your connection with them—they are actually now able to understand you more than they ever did before!

○ ○ ○

In the next chapter I will explain how to receive feedback from your deceased loved ones after you have written your letters to them. I'll talk about how meditation will help you to connect with them, how they may come through to you, how to become more aware of signs, and more. If you feel you are unable to connect with your deceased loved ones yourself, I provide a section on how to find a good medium who will be able to do it for you.

❧ ◎ ❧

getting feedback from your deceased loved ones

After you have written your letters, your deceased loved ones may attempt to contact you to let you know that they have witnessed your efforts. This chapter will show you how to look for signs and receive the messages that your loved ones may be giving you to let you know that they are around.

The Essence of Our Immortal Spirit Is Energy

I'm truly convinced that anyone who is interested can learn how to communicate with deceased loved ones. Before I explain how to do this, however, I would first like to talk about the essence of our souls. The bottom line is that a person's energy continues to exist even after it leaves the physical body. For people who need a logical explanation, as stated in the law of the conservation of energy in physics: the total amount of energy remains constant. In other words, energy can be converted from one form to another, but it cannot be created or destroyed. Therefore, the energy of the spirit always was and always will be. It continues even after physical death, when it just changes from one form to another.

I like to compare the energy of one's soul to water. If you place water in a glass and leave it in the middle of the room, it eventually evaporates. In other words, the water still exists, but it eventually evolves into a different form; it no longer is confined to the glass but is now able to permeate the room. The same is true with one's soul after physical death. It leaves the body but continues to exist without it. This energy was limited to the body before, but it is free now.

Loved Ones Come Through with Their Same Personalities

Our loved ones' personalities do not change after they leave this world. For example, people who were loud still come through as a huge presence, people who were quiet have a soft energy, people who were funny are still comical, and so on. In other words, their energy is the same as it always was.

When my clients want to know what loved ones say about something that is going on in their lives, I always ask them if they would listen to their loved ones when they were alive. If the answer is no, I tell them that their loved ones don't know everything just because they are out of their bodies. It takes time on the other side to learn and advance to higher levels.

Also, people who have recently crossed over are often very anxious to let living loved ones know that they are all right. They usually stay around and watch over the living for a while to make sure that they are okay, and try to make it known that they are with them.

After some time, their spirits move on and evolve, and they are not as determined to stay around as when they first left their bodies. They are now acclimated to the other side and are learning different things to advance to the next level.

Even after your departed loved ones have grown accustomed to the other side and moved on, however, they are still able to come through to let you know that they are okay. The feeling of urgency to communicate with you, though, is not as strong. At this time, it is therefore a little harder, but not impossible, to connect with their energy.

Make the Connection Through Meditation

If you are really serious about connecting with the other side, the most important advice I have for you is to learn how to meditate. During meditation, you are quieting your mind so that you can listen to all that is. Praying is talking to God, whereas meditating is *listening* to Him. As in any relationship, it certainly isn't ideal if you just speak and don't listen to the other party.

Try to set aside 10 to 20 minutes each day with just the intention of quieting your thoughts. It's important to realize that you shouldn't expect messages during meditation. The true benefit of meditating is that you are learning to clear your mind on demand. If you do this often enough, you will become very sensitive to energies around you; then, when you feel that your loved ones are around, you'll be able to quickly go back to that quiet state to receive any messages they are giving you.

Before You Begin to Meditate

It's best to meditate at the same place and time each day. It's okay if you can't do this every day, but at least attempt to be consistent. You should also feel comfortable during meditation, so remove anything you are wearing that is tight or binding. Choose a block of time when you won't be interrupted, and find a quiet space that makes you feel calm and relaxed.

It is also important to create a nice, peaceful environment *around* you. You may want to turn on soothing music in the background and light wonderfully scented candles. You can also call upon angels and ascended masters to raise the vibration of the room.

Simple Ways to Meditate

One easy way to meditate is to breathe deeply in and out. Begin counting your exhalations, and when you get to your tenth one, you may start the whole process again. This method is very simple; it should end most of your mental chatter and allow you to stay focused on the moment.

Another easy way to meditate is to stare at a lit candle. When you can't keep your eyes open anymore, simply close them. Within a few seconds, you will begin to see the flame in your closed eyelids. When the flame disappears, open your eyes and stare at the candle once again. Then, repeat the process a few more times.

Remember, don't expect to receive messages during the quiet time. The meditation is simply to open your senses and intuition to receive messages more directly and clearly when they *do* come in your everyday life. (I meditate every morning before my appointments, to open myself up to receive messages from deceased loved ones later in the day.)

If you find it difficult to quiet your mind, you may want to purchase a guided meditation CD that will take you through relaxation exercises. Taking the time to relax while listening to the CD will help you to get into "meditation mode." After doing the guided meditation daily for a month or so, try to move on to emptying your mind without the CD. (For more details about meditation and how to connect with the other side, you may want to read my book *The Rainbow Follows the Storm: How to Obtain Inner Peace by Connecting with Angels and Deceased Loved Ones.*)

Make the Connection by Becoming More Aware of Signs

Besides meditation, there are a number of things you can do to connect with your deceased loved ones. The most important is to become more aware of signs. Please know that your loved ones want to connect with you as much as you want to connect with them, and they are probably trying to give you signs to let you know that they are around you.

For example, if a car cuts you off, look at the license plate. It may be your loved one's name or another significant detail about that person. Also, notice special songs that come on at just the right time. Become more aware of scents around you that logically shouldn't be there, such as your loved one's perfume, cigar or cigarette smoke, or deodorant. Also, pay attention to unusual items that you repeatedly find, such as coins or feathers.

Here is an example from my own life. The last day my mother was conscious before she died, she was telling my family and me that she was sorry she wasn't able to buy Christmas presents for anyone. (She couldn't because she was too weak!) She promised to make it up to all of us later. Of course, we told her that it was okay and not to worry about it.

She still wasn't happy about not giving us any-thing, and turned to me and asked, "Karen, may I borrow seven dollars? Don't worry, I'll pay you back."

"Of course," I told her, and quickly grabbed seven singles out of my wallet and gave them to her.

She took each dollar bill and handed them out to all seven of us in the room while proudly saying, "One for you, one for you, one for you . . .," until all seven dollars were handed out, and she was satisfied that she was able to give us all something that day after all.

After she passed away, I forgot all about this inci-dent—until I started finding dollar bills in the most random places. One day I found one on my car seat. The same day I found one on the floor in my waiting room and then another in my office. The next day I found one on the floor in my house.

Just as I wondered why I was finding all these one-dollar bills, I felt my mom's presence come into the room, and she gently said, "Hi sweetheart. I *told* you I'd pay you back. I love you with all my heart."

I began to cry, and answered, "Ma, you didn't have to pay me back. I love *you* with all my heart."

And just when I thought it had all stopped, about a month later a friend of mine made me a "shadow box" that contained my mom's pictures and other memorabilia. In the box she included a single dollar bill. She said she didn't know why, but she knew she needed to include it with everything.

I can't wait to see where I'll find the remaining dollars, not because I want the money back but because I love receiving these amazing signs from my mother. It's so comforting to know that she really is still around and continues to watch over me.

(By the way, as stated earlier, the personalities of our deceased loved ones continue even after they leave their bodies. When my mom was here on earth, she always made sure to pay off her debts. It's no surprise to me at all that she's continuing to do this from the other side.)

⊡ ⊡ ⊡

Another big way that our deceased loved ones let us know they are around is by using their energy to briefly go inside a bird, butterfly, dragonfly, ladybug, or any other animal. You won't have to look for them, because they will find *you*. Such was the case when Rosemarie's beloved father decided to let her know he was there; he came to her as a persistent, beautiful butterfly on the Jersey shore.

"As I took a stroll on the beach in late September, in my thoughts I asked my dad—who had died a few years earlier—to hook me up with some sea glass. I also asked for him to stay with me, because I missed him so much. Just as I finished thinking this, a beautiful butterfly landed beneath my feet. When I bent down, it allowed me to pick it up. Then I started to talk to this beautiful creature. As I held it in my hand, it spread its wings and just remained there. I was able to pet its beautiful wings, and I also stroked its long body. When I began walking, the wind started to blow, and then, all of a sudden, the butterfly decided to fly to my chest. He remained there the whole walk back and didn't move. I then walked up to the boardwalk and sat on the bench. I started to talk to the butterfly, and it went from my chest to my hair, back to my chest, and then into my hand.

"As I had it in my hand, two men looked over and started to walk toward me. One of them said, 'Hey, you caught a butterfly!' I responded with a smile and a giggle, 'No, actually it caught me!' They proceeded to walk closer, and I still had the butterfly with me in my hand. The butterfly then moved to my chest. One man asked if I was going to keep it, and I told him no, that it was free to go whenever it chose to. After that, the man asked if I was going to hurt it. 'No,' I said, 'of course not; it's beautiful!' Then the man started to walk a bit closer to me, and all of a sudden, the butterfly flew up to the sky and just vanished.

"I left that beach and proceeded to go to another beach. When I arrived there, I started to meditate, and as I looked up, the same butterfly was fluttering all around. I didn't get to hold it this time though.

"Finally, it was time to go, and as I drove on the Toms River Bridge, I had the sunroof open. As I looked up, right above my sunroof was the same butterfly!

"Since that experience, I have been seeing butterflies of that same color all around. Karen gave me a book called *Inspiration,* by Dr. Wayne Dyer, who had a story similar to mine, and the picture he used on the cover reflected that of my butterfly. I can't stop thinking about it and how awesome that experience was for me. I will never forget it! It was a true sign that my dad was with me. What a unique experience!

"Little did I know that my dad was preparing me for the crossing over of my mom a few months later. Karen has since helped me to see that they both are okay and around when I need them. Just knowing that they are with me brings me so much comfort. I am so thankful for this whole experience."

How wonderful it was that Rosemarie's father came to his beloved daughter as a butterfly, not only to let her know that he was okay, but also to let her know that her mother would also be all right when she made her transition and joined him a few months after his glorious appearance on the beach. He had truly given her a magnificent gift that she will always cherish on that cool, breezy day in September on the New Jersey shore!

Make the Connection by Using Dreams

Another very good way to receive messages is to ask your loved one to come to you in a dream. Just be persistent, and it will happen. You'll realize you have experienced a true visitation when you wake up and know without a doubt that your loved one was there. The dream is usually very peaceful and never frightening, so don't worry. (Fear-provoking dreams come from the subconscious mind, not from your departed loved one.) When you have a true visitation from your loved one in a dream, it is more vivid and real than an ordinary dream, and you will probably remember it in detail many years later.

You will also need to wake up after such a dream, or else you won't remember it. Therefore, when you ask your deceased loved ones to come to you in a dream, make sure to tell them to wake you up afterward.

I did this with my own mom. After she passed, I had been asking her to come to me in a dream, and to let me hear her voice one more time. One day I stayed home and was able to take a nap. While I was asleep, I dreamed that I was in a crowded place. All of a sudden, my mother's voice came over the loudspeaker, and she said, "I have an important announcement! I have an important announcement! I am here, and I am okay!"

After she spoke, I inquired, "Who are you with?" She responded in a very low voice with a name I couldn't hear. Then I asked her to turn up the volume and tell me again. She responded softly, "Nannie." Nannie is what I called my maternal grandmother.

Then the phone rang and awakened me, which enabled me to remember the dream.

When I woke up, I felt as if I had won the lottery. The dream was so real, and I *knew* my Mom had truly paid me a visit. It was the best gift she could have ever given me!

Staying Open to Telepathic Messages

Finally, please realize that your loved one may give you messages telepathically—as thoughts and feelings. If you randomly feel or think of your loved one, chances are, that person is there.

The key to interpreting whether it is your own thought or your loved one's thought is to backtrack to what was going on inside your head prior to your thinking of that person. Did you see something that reminded you of your loved one, or did something just *pop* into your head for no apparent reason? If it just popped into your head, your loved one is probably making his or her presence known to you.

Do be kind to yourself and don't try too hard. As a matter of fact, straining to receive messages doesn't work, so just allow it to occur. When you least expect it, someday, in some way, you *will* get the message you have always wanted.

Making That Connection Through Someone Else: Finding a Good Medium

When all else fails, and you still don't feel confident in your ability to communicate with your deceased loved ones, you can always go to a medium who can make the connection for you. The best way to find a good one is to obtain a recommendation from someone who has been to the medium. You probably wouldn't look for a doctor, lawyer, or anyone else in the yellow pages, so you shouldn't seek a psychic in this way either.

When Visiting a Medium . . .

When they make an appointment with a medium, many people ask me what they need to do to prepare for the session. The answer is quite simple: if you want to connect with someone who has crossed, mentally ask the person with whom you want to connect to please come to the session. You may also bring a picture or something significant that the person owned, but that's not necessary. What it really boils down to is the intent to connect.

When a Psychic Says Something That Scares You

I don't believe in coincidences, and something strange happened to me as I was writing this chapter. A well-intentioned acquaintance said she "saw" that something bad was going to happen to me, and she went into detail about it. Right away, I knew that this was *not* going to happen to me, but I immediately went within myself to see why the Universe was pushing her to tell me this. I then understood that I needed to share the following information with you. If a psychic comes out and says that something bad is going to happen to you and it doesn't resonate with you, do not take it seriously! Your thoughts create your reality, and you can actually make things happen by your *belief* that it will happen. If you are fearful that something *possibly* will happen and you give it enough energy, you can create the very thing that you fear. Thank goodness, I know about this concept, and from the start, I gave my friend's pronouncement no energy.

If a psychic or well-intentioned friend comes right out with the claim of "seeing" a horrible thing, don't listen. Real psychics know how our thoughts create reality, and will tell you in a nice way how to prevent something that they feel may be in your path—with no fear involved. They will peacefully guide you through how *not* to make it happen. It is this guidance that will prevent the negative situation from manifesting.

If No One Comes Through

Although it doesn't happen often, there may be times when no one comes through. I have found that there may be a number of reasons for this. For example, a person who has recently crossed is usually more anxious to come through than one who has been gone a long time. If someone has been gone for a long time, that person may have moved on to another level on the other side or may have reincarnated. Another reason someone can't come through is that this person is just not in the room at the time of the reading. A psychic cannot make someone appear, so if your loved one is not in the room, the psychic won't be able to pick up on that person's energy.

Another explanation for someone not coming through is that either that person's energy is very low, or your own energy is low. Remember, a psychic is reading energy, so it may be even more difficult to pick up on energy if you and the deceased person are both quiet. This doesn't mean it can't be done; it's just harder.

Still another reason why someone may not come through is that you don't want this loved one to give you messages. At such times, some healing may need to take place before communication can occur. I recently had a client come in for an appointment and say that she had told her father not to come through, because she was so angry at him. It was no surprise then, when he didn't come with messages for her.

Of course, there may be still other reasons why a deceased loved one may not come through. A psychic may be "off" on a particular day, trying too hard, or unable to fully trust the information being received.

If the medium is a reputable one, try to be open to whoever or whatever comes through. Sometimes people on the other side have a different agenda than you do, so be willing to accept whatever occurs. Always remember, too, that your loved ones are okay, and if you are persistent, they will definitely let you know one way or another that they are with you, even if they weren't able to make themselves known during the reading.

◙ ◙ ◙

I hope you now understand how to get feedback from your deceased loved ones, whether or not you've written letters to them. They truly are all right, and they want you to be, too!

In the next chapter, I will explain that letter writing is not the only way to see through the eyes of others, and I will talk about a number of other things you can do to see "the bigger picture" to create peace in your relationships.

❦ ◙ ❦

other ways to see through the eyes of another

Writing letters is not the only way to see through another's eyes. You may not want to write letters or even have the time to do so, and that's okay! The point is to see the "bigger picture" with every interaction you have. As a matter of fact, it's important to do this even if you *have* written these letters. It's something you can learn to do moment to moment, day to day. And it's very simple: just really pay attention to all of the people around you!

Become Aware of Everyone You Encounter

Take notice of the people in your path. Make each person's life a little better just because you're in it. Remember that no one is more or less significant than another. Whether it is a person who is driving down the highway, one who is pushing a cart in the supermarket, or someone at work, the other person deserves to be treated with love and respect. Start seeing that we truly are all one, and sense God within every person and animal you encounter.

— **Just tell them how you feel.** Allow your loved ones to know how much they mean to you. Simply tell them how you feel and what you admire about them. Call them, e-mail them, text them, or do it in person. If people are being kind, thank them and acknowledge what they have done. That will encourage them to continue to be caring, and will, in turn, create a ripple effect of spreading even more kindness around the world.

— **Really listen to others.** Look others in the eye when they are speaking to you, and really *listen* to them. Try not to jump in with your experiences until they are finished with what they are saying.

Allow everyone to know that they are being heard and are significant—because they are!

— **Return calls and e-mails.** Return phone calls and e-mails in a timely manner. Someone may be waiting for you to return a call or e-mail. If you don't respond, that person may feel regarded as insignificant by you. Try to think how *you* would feel if the people in your life didn't respond to your messages. You wouldn't like it, so don't do that to others.

— **Offer your time.** Set aside time in your busy schedule to let your loved ones know that they are special. Get together "just because" or to acknowledge important events such as birthdays, accomplishments, and so on. Don't put it off for when you think you'll be less busy. Your loved ones may not be around at a later date and you will have missed an opportunity to let them know that you really do care.

— **Extend your kindness to people who serve you.** Treat the people who serve you with compassion. For those who are working for tips, try to leave a larger tip than is expected. If you have time, leave a little note of appreciation with your tip. Smile when people are serving you. Praise them and let their managers know they are doing a great job. Treat all of the people who serve or work for you just as you would like to be treated, and see how you can make their day a little brighter.

— **Speak well of others.** Say kind things to others about the people in your life. Your positive words may get back to your loved ones, and you will truly have made their day. Even if they don't consciously know what you have said, they will feel it energetically. It will also benefit *you* when you spread the light; because of the Law of Attraction, you will be creating more positive people and experiences around you as well.

— **Share and offer your help.** Share whatever you can with others, whether it is your services, material objects, or anything else. Offer to help *before* the other person asks. Many times our friends or family don't want to bother us and won't ask if they need something. Also, when you help another, make sure you do it lovingly. The other person will be able to feel it if you are only doing it because you think you have to.

Be There for Yourself as Well

It's extremely important to be there for yourself as well. Say no if you can't do what someone is asking of you. Take the time to enjoy the things you love to do. Honor yourself and acknowledge your amazing qualities.

The whole point is to see yourself from a broader perspective, as if you were *someone else* trying to make *your* life a little better. Truly understand that you alone are responsible for making all your dreams come true.

Remember, it's the little things that matter. Think of ways to make everyone's day more special, including your own. Really notice the people who cross your path and see how you are affecting them. Notice how you are treating yourself as well. Remember, you are just as important as anyone else and need to be treated with respect. By extending compassion to everyone, including yourself, you will be creating peace in your life and in all the lives around you.

an ongoing
PROCESS

after you complete your life review

In writing every single letter, your intention should be to obtain peace in your life and in the lives around you—right here, right now. And because of your intention, you should receive exactly what you have requested. After you have written your letters, your life will gradually begin to shift into a new, more positive reality. Of course, you will receive different responses depending on the type of letter you have written.

Maintain the Peace You Have Created

Remember, you may not be able to change what is going on around you, but you *can* change the way you react to it. If you strive for peace in every situation, you will experience more of it in your life. Please understand that it doesn't end with the letter writing; this absolutely is an ongoing process. Intentions must be followed by actions to show the recipients of your letters that you truly want to maintain peace with them.

New issues certainly will arise as time goes by. You may change. The recipients of your letters may change. So many things may come to pass! Just remember to continue to keep that peace with everyone, including yourself, throughout your years here on earth.

Leave no words unspoken to the people in your life. Live each day being kind to those who cross your path, and always try to see everything from the other person's point of view. When you look at everything from this higher perspective, you will be able to understand the people around you a lot better.

I'm not saying it will always be easy. Sometimes, on the surface it may seem so difficult that you won't know how you will be able to do it. You may agonize over various situations and even lose sleep over what you need to do. However, because your intention is pure, you should eventually figure out how to obtain peace in each situation. At that point, just carry out whatever needs to be done to obtain this peace.

Love and Honor Yourself

As stated in earlier chapters, it's crucial to love and honor yourself. When you truly comprehend that you are just as significant as everyone else, and when you do whatever it takes to keep the peace within you, your whole life will take off in a more positive direction.

This may mean that it is just easier to stay away from certain people because of the negativity they bring into your life. At this point, please listen to your inner guidance. While you may not be able to change others, you *can* change how you respond to their negativity. In some cases, staying away from them may be the best solution. Remember, your needs are just as important as those of the other person, and obtaining peace should be your ultimate goal.

Always stand up for yourself, and don't wait for someone else to do it for you. Really pay attention to your wants and needs. Before you get out of bed each morning, ask how you can create the perfect day for yourself. Then follow up with whatever needs to be done to make that happen!

Most important, always continue to maintain this newfound serenity in your life; attempt to find tranquility in every situation, regardless of what is happening around you. As Wayne Dyer has stated so perfectly, "When you change the way you look at things, the things you look at change." This is so true!

Finding Peace Within at All Times

It's very easy to feel peaceful when everything is going well in your life. However, when things aren't going well, the key to maintaining serenity is to try to refocus your thoughts and look at the positive side in every (yes, every!) situation. When you begin to look on the bright side of every situation, you will, in turn, attract more positive situations into your life. Sometimes the transformation takes a certain amount of time, while at other times it can be instantaneous. In other words, when you see the best in every situation, the universe will bring you more things to be grateful for—every time!

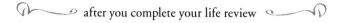

Such was the case when I sat down to write this book and ran into a few obstacles along the way. In essence, I had to set aside certain days to write, twelve months ahead of time, because of my busy schedule at work. When this prescheduled writing time finally arrived, I was anxious to get started, and even moved to another office to have a quieter place to write. However, when I was all set to begin writing, I encountered some unexpected complications. Looking back now, I see that everything happened for a reason—so that I could fully understand just how important it was to continue to try to keep the peace within, no matter what was going on outside of me. Oh, what a lesson that was!

Just as I was taking my laptop out of its case to begin writing, a group of workers pulled up in front of my office and started setting up their equipment on the roof. As soon as I found out they were going to replace the roof, I began to worry about how loud they would be. Unfortunately, within a short period of time, they began making so much noise that I couldn't concentrate on what I had intended to write. Instead, I just typed out my frustrations:

"I am sitting in my office here, trying to write, while crews of men are using blowtorches and drilling my roof; and I must say: they are loud! I have tried going into different rooms to see if the noise level was better somewhere else. I tried playing soft harp music on my CD player. I tried using the white noise mode on my sound-effects machine; but I *still* hear the constant, loud droning of the machinery.

"Okay, I'm the type who needs silence (or close to it) to write or to get work done. So I ask myself, *What is the message here?* I set aside this day over a year ago so that I could write, so I definitely need to use this time wisely.

"What is the Universe telling me? I realize that every single thing that goes on in my life is a creation of my thoughts. What the heck could this mean?

"Because I can't think clearly at this moment, the only message I'm getting—loud (no pun intended) and clear—is that in order to create peace in your life, it really doesn't matter what is going on outside of yourself. The true peace must come from *within*.

"So, exactly how can we maintain peace within when the outside world is screaming of unrest? As I sit here now, I am trying to focus on the beautiful harp music I have playing in the background. I turned the music up to drown out the noise, but that has just created further turmoil in the room. I can't meditate, because it will be impossible to experience silence.

"Focusing on the positive aspects could be the way to go, I say to myself. It's difficult at first, but I know this change in awareness will trigger more positive thoughts, which in turn will trigger a more peaceful feeling. I literally have to force myself to do this. There is drilling on one side of the roof, and there are men walking on the other side. Through all of this, there is a continuous, loud, droning sound of machinery outside.

"I try to stay positive. At first it is difficult, but I force myself, because I know this will change everything.

"My thoughts begin to shift. I realize the crew is fixing the roof so that there will be no more leaks. They are protecting and sealing my office. This is a *good* thing.

"Then I glance up and see such a peaceful, beautiful room. I focus on the fact that I just moved into this new, larger office three weeks ago, and I love entering this haven each day.

"Because I'm sitting in the waiting room (it's a bit quieter than my office), I see the beautiful mural of cherubs that one of my clients painted on my wall. Directly in the center of the mural are huge angel wings with a magnificent rainbow going right through them. I try focusing on this, and I see such beauty in it all.

"The distractions in the background are beginning to be less noticeable than they were before, and I'm feeling much better. I'm now even able to smell the lilac scent of the candle I have burning on the coffee table. The music seems to be the dominant noise I hear now. How is that possible?

"I can understand the meaning of all of this now. Life is full of distractions that may shift our attention to what we don't want instead of what we want. Sometimes these distractions are hard to ignore, but it is during the most difficult times that we must try harder to stay focused on our intentions. Sometimes we literally have to force ourselves to see and feel beyond what is going on outside of ourselves to feel the peace and love *within* ourselves.

"I truly am thankful for the whole experience, because it has taught me this great lesson. When I began to shift my focus onto the positive aspects of all that was happening, I was able to see and feel more of what I wanted instead of what I didn't want. Although it took a lot of patience and perseverance, in the end, I was able to see how important it is to perceive the love and peace in *everything!*"

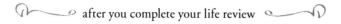

You Can Do It, Too!

So, you're saying to yourself, *how does that relate to me?* It's very simple. You, too, can either try to refocus your thoughts on something that makes you feel better and is totally unrelated to what is happening, or put all your attention on any positive aspect of whatever you are experiencing. It also helps to write down the positive qualities that are coming from the situation at hand.

Remember, *you* are the only one who can break away from those bad thoughts and see the bright side in every situation. When you can do it during the most difficult times, you certainly will be able to do it at any other time too. The key is to think about what you *want,* not what you don't want. If you think about what you want, you will receive more of what you want. If you keep focusing on what you don't want, you will continue to receive things you don't want.

Just as I was finishing up this chapter, I felt guided to call Sue, a client who had recently come in for an appointment, to see how she was doing. She informed me that she had just found out that her son Daniel needed to get a hearing aid. Of course, her response was a normal one; she was concerned for her child and was very upset.

Immediately, I knew that I was supposed to remind her to stay positive, especially now. Even though this felt like another obstacle in her precious son's life (he had already been through a number of health-related issues), she needed to see the good in it all. I told her it was wonderful that his hearing was now going to be restored. It was also great that he didn't have to go through any more of those dreaded medical tests.

After talking with her for a while, I was pleased that her energy gradually shifted from despair to relief when she understood that her son would be much better off with the hearing aid than without it. While this probably won't be the last negative situation Sue will ever encounter in her life, she now truly understands just how important it is to see the best in absolutely everything that comes her way.

◎ ◎ ◎

Although you, just like Sue, may not be able to change what's going on in the world around you, you *can* change what's going on *inside* of you. When you learn to look for the positive in every situation, no matter what is happening, you truly will begin

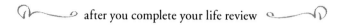

to feel so much better. Try it, and you will see that it really works!

summing it all up: seeing through the eyes of others

As a psychic medium, I often feel the emotions of people around me as if they were my own, so understanding another person's point of view is usually very easy for me to do. I realize it may not be this effortless for everyone, but I'm absolutely sure that if you can at least *try* to see through the eyes of others and respond to them in peace, your whole life will change for the better.

Writing a letter is one of the best ways to express your positive feelings to your loved ones. In this way, you are taking the time to express exactly what you want to say, and the recipients of your letters will also have a tangible piece of evidence of your intended peace with them that they can look over whenever they choose. Remember that following up on your positive intentions is just as important as the letters themselves, so creating peace with those around you should be an ongoing process. Do whatever needs to be done to maintain positive relationships with everyone—and always include yourself in that equation! Sometimes it will be a very difficult thing to do, but it will always be worth it.

As situations evolve and you observe others doing things that you don't understand, sit back and try to see where they are coming from before criticizing or attacking them. Peace is not obtained by pointing your finger and saying it's someone else's fault. It's about taking responsibility for your actions in every situation.

Here are a few essential points: First, please don't look to others to change to fit your needs, because they may never do so! They may just not be in alignment with your energy, and that's okay. We are all where we need to be at any given time.

Also, this whole process is not only about making others feel better, because they may *never* feel

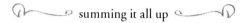

better. The whole purpose of seeing through the eyes of others is not to please everyone else; it's to obtain peace within *yourself*.

Finally, try to understand that while you open your heart and strive for peace with those around you, don't always expect others to send that love back to you, for they may not be able to do so. In reality, we are all one anyway, and the loving, positive energy that you give to another will definitely return to you on some level.

The Importance of Loving Yourself

While sending love to those around you is essential to obtaining peace in your life, loving yourself is always just as significant. Remember, seeing everything through the eyes of others doesn't mean putting yourself last; it actually means putting yourself *first!* After you begin to respond to your own needs, you will actually be in a much better position to help others.

As soon as you wake up in the morning, ask yourself what you can do to make your day easier, and then do whatever it takes to make that happen. Observe everything through grateful eyes as you go about your daily chores. Keep a constant, loving inner dialogue, and use positive affirmations throughout each hour. Attempt to see the good in every situation you encounter. Remember that you can always learn something positive, even in the midst of chaos.

To help you fully understand what I mean by all of this, I am going to re-create for you a typical day of keeping the peace amid the unwanted twists and turns of life. I chose to write about normal events that happened to me on the day I was writing this chapter.

Creating a Peaceful Day by Seeing the Bigger Picture

As soon as I opened my eyes in the morning, I began thinking about what I needed to do for the day. Thankfully, I took the day off to write, so I didn't have appointments scheduled. I thought about how I was still planning to go into my office so that I could return phone calls and e-mails, and then write when that was all done. I mentally planned everything out in my mind and was excited to finally be having a nice, relaxing day. Then, I stepped out of my bed and began to think about everything I was grateful for, remembering even minor things in my life that I sometimes take for granted.

After finishing my morning chores, I packed up and was ready to leave. However, when I opened the door to the garage, I saw my son Tim, who should have been at school already, still sitting in his car. He told me he'd locked his car keys, his baseball uniform, and all of his school supplies in the trunk and wasn't able to go to school or drive his car.

As one would expect, Tim was a bit agitated, but he told me he'd left another set of keys at his dad's house. Thankfully, I didn't have any appointments, so it wasn't a problem for me to drive him there to get his keys. However, once we reached his dad's house, he couldn't find the keys anywhere.

At this point, inner guidance peacefully told me to have him call the dealership where he'd bought his car to ask if they had an extra key to his trunk. They said yes, but he would have to bring his ID and registration. This meant that I had to drive my son back to my house, where this documentation was. When we arrived at my house, I called the school to tell them he was going to be late because of all that had happened.

We then hopped into my car and drove to the dealership, which was about a half hour away. Luckily, they were able to make a copy of the key to his trunk, and of course, we were both relieved.

Throughout this ordeal, I tried to see the bright side of everything; I didn't have any appointments scheduled for the day, which was rare, so I didn't have to worry about getting to my office. Regardless of the circumstances, it was great to have this extra time with my son. Also, when something out of the ordinary occurs, I always look within myself to see the purpose of what has transpired. What did Tim or I need to learn from all of this? Certainly, Tim learned to always have an extra set of keys somewhere, just in case this ever happened again. More important, however, we both learned patience; being impatient or worrying would have made everything so much worse.

As an added bonus, my son and I also shared a couple of laughs during our ride together. On the way to the dealership, I had just been explaining to Tim that every time the song "White Horse" by Laid Back came on my iPod, a horse always "appeared" somewhere. He didn't think much of it, but as soon as the song came on, we passed a restaurant with a huge—and I do mean *huge*—statue of a horse on its roof! We both started to laugh so hard that all the tension within us was immediately released. If this wasn't enough, as I was driving home, the iPod just

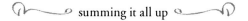
stopped, and then it fast-forwarded to a beautiful song that we both needed to hear at the time.

Despite the unusual circumstances of the day, it was really great that Tim and I, who are both always on the go, were able to spend this time together. As a by-product, he also was able to get a better understanding of the crazy things that happen in my world. When I looked at him from the corner of my eye and saw him laughing, I knew it was all worth it.

After we arrived home, he was able to use the new key to get his belongings out of the trunk. At that point, all the so-called problems had been resolved; I gave him a hug and told him I loved him, and he was off to another day.

Because I didn't want to waste any more time traveling, I then decided to work from home. Surprisingly, I was glad about the way everything had transpired, because I ended up having a wonderful day with my animals in my comfy home, doing whatever I wanted to do and writing whenever the mood hit me. For the remaining hours in the day, I attempted to think positively and continued to keep a peaceful inner dialogue about everything I encountered. As always, whenever I felt a knot in my stomach, I repeated my favorite Louise Hay affirmation, "All is well in my world." (Whenever I repeat this mantra for a few minutes, my whole energy shifts, and I feel *so* much better!)

Then, in the late afternoon, I went to the supermarket to get a few things, and as always, I made sure to really notice everyone around me. I pushed my cart to the side of the lane to get out of the other shoppers' way when I stopped to look at items I needed; I made sure my supermarket card and money were ready before I checked out so that no one had to wait for me; I helped bag my items so that the clerk didn't have to do it; and so on. Although all these things may seem insignificant, they meant a lot to the people around me in the store.

Afterward, I went to my son's baseball game. As I was watching his team play, I was aware of the feelings of the players on *both* teams and their families. While I clapped for those on my son's team whenever they made good plays, I remained quiet when things didn't go well or if errors were made. I simply enjoyed the game and proudly watched my son and both teams play ball.

When the game was over, I went home to make a quick dinner for my son and me. After I cleaned up, because I was so tired, I decided to relax for the rest of the evening. When I went to bed early that night, I mentally went through a mini life review to

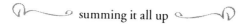

see how I had affected each person and animal I encountered. I spent extra time on this review to make
sure that I had treated myself well too. For the most
part, I was satisfied with what I had accomplished
that day, and I made a mental note of some of the
things that I could have done better.

How You Can Do It

You can truly make a difference in your life and
in the lives of others simply by viewing everything
from a higher perspective. Try to see the bright side
of every situation that comes your way. Live every
day being kind and helping each person who crosses
your path. Attempt to see everything from the other
person's point of view. Always remember to respect
yourself as well! When you truly comprehend that
you are just as significant as everyone else, your
whole life will change. If you remember to love yourself and others unconditionally, you will be vibrating at a much higher level. It is at this point that you
will truly be able to create peace in your life and in
the world around you.

Perform a mini life review at least once a week,
seeing the broader picture of how you have affected others, yourself, animals, and nature. This will

give you a clue as to how you are doing. Sadly, most people won't fully realize how they have affected the world until it is too late, that is, after they have crossed over to the other side. It is then that they will decide to "do it better the next time."

How great would it be if you could get it right *this* time around? This not only would create peace within yourself and with those around you, but also would begin a ripple effect that could actually make the world a more positive place for everyone. You would be creating heaven on earth, right here, right now! And how wonderful is that?

I'm concluding this part of the book with Saint Francis of Assisi's prayer that says it all.

Lord, make me an instrument of your peace.
Where there is hatred, let me sow love;
Where there is injury, pardon;
Where there is doubt, faith;
Where there is despair, hope;
Where there is darkness, light;
And where there is sadness, joy.
Oh Divine Master, grant that I may not so much seek
To be consoled as to console;
To be understood as to understand;
To be loved as to love;

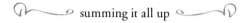 summing it all up

For it is in giving that we receive;
It is in pardoning that we are pardoned;
And it is in dying that we are born to eternal life.

And so it is.

⊡ ⊡ ⊡

May you continue to see the light of God in every person and everything you encounter. Many blessings to you!

�֍ ⊡ ✎

afterword

As a medium, I continually receive proof that our souls never die. After your loved ones leave the earthly plane, they want you to know that they are still around you and are okay. They are anxious to tell you that they are aware of what's going on around you, and they sometimes reveal things *you* aren't even aware of yet. If you aren't able to "pick up on" what they are saying, they often give you signs that you won't be able to ignore.

Because they have left the physical body, they can see all things from a higher perspective, even seeing through your eyes exactly how they have affected you. Many times they feel that it's too late to make things right, when it really isn't.

Since I have been able to grasp their concept of seeing everything from a higher perspective, my life has changed so much. I try (and sometimes, believe me, it's hard!) to live each day and see things from the other person's point of view. And you know what? I can honestly say that my life has changed so much for the better because of it. I have truly obtained an abundance of peace within myself after extending this peace and love to everyone else. My goal was to share this knowledge with you.

Please remember that the true purpose of your life is to recognize and work toward unconditional love. *You* can be the peace that you desire to see in the world. It is your birthright. You are a spiritual being having a human experience, not the other way around. You are Divine; you are love; you are light!

❧ ◉ ❧

appendix

Messages from
"the Other Side" and More

In this appendix, I include some stories from my readings that will help you to more fully understand what happens to us after we leave the body. In the following stories, I've incorporated the answers to questions my clients frequently ask me. As a common thread to all of these stories, you will see that our departed loved ones are usually very anxious to let us know they are around us and are okay.

When Someone Dies Unexpectedly

Many people are concerned about whether a spirit is at peace after an unexpected death, such as an accident, murder, or suicide. The answer is quite simple: The soul of the person who has crossed over is usually fine and wants loved ones to know this. In the case of a suicide, the person feels the pain that this experience has caused loved ones, and usually wants to express remorse to those who remain for causing them such sorrow. Once that connection is made with loved ones and apologies are accepted, the spirit is able to move on and evolve to another level. What the deceased one realizes is that living loved ones are also sorry, because they feel that they could have done something to prevent this death. When all is said and done, after the deceased and the living have made peace with each other, the one who has crossed over usually states that loved ones could *not* have prevented the suicide. At this time, they are all finally able to move on peacefully with this comforting, newfound knowledge.

Whenever a death occurs unexpectedly because of a murder or an accident, the deceased person is usually very determined to contact living loved ones to let them know everything is okay. The message is usually urgent and one that is hard to ignore. Such was the case with Ryan, whose life ended much too soon, when he accidentally drowned while taking a walk on the beach after leaving a party.

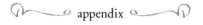 appendix

Young Man Reaches Out from the Other Side after Being Reported Missing

As I was watching my son play baseball, I spotted my friend Rose coming toward me, carrying a man's jacket. She seemed distraught, and I immediately asked her what was wrong. She told me that her nephew Ryan had been missing after going to a party a few weeks earlier, and she wanted me to hold his coat to see if I could pick up on anything about him. After giving Rose a hug, I told her I would take the coat home to see if I could "feel" anything from it.

Right away, I sensed so much sad energy around the coat. I'm sure I was picking up on how distraught Ryan's family was, and not on Ryan, at that point. I began to meditate and tried to discount what I was getting. I believed Ryan was in spirit, but I wasn't sure what had happened. As a mother of a boy the same age as Ryan, I didn't want to accept what I was receiving. Ryan had crossed over, and I didn't want to be the one to tell his family. I just couldn't do it. What if what I was receiving was a mistake and I was picking up on another young man who had crossed over?

I told the young man that I just couldn't tell his family what had happened unless he gave me very specific messages that it was truly him. I then went on to tell him that as soon as they found him, he should come to me immediately, and I would relay his messages to his loved ones then.

One day, while I was at my friend Rose's house, I asked her to call her sister Mary Jane, Ryan's mom, because I had begun to see events clairvoyantly as we were talking about Ryan. After Rose called her sister and I took the phone to speak to her, I told Mary Jane that I saw a picture of a long stick where the river meets another body of water. I insinuated what I knew, but just couldn't come out and say that Ryan was in spirit. I do think she understood what I was saying though. A few more messages came through as well, and after a while, we ended our conversation.

About a month had passed and while I was at home talking to my son Tim, I felt Ryan enter the room with an urgent energy, shouting, "Call my mom *now!*"

Of course, I immediately called Mary Jane, who coincidentally had been visiting her sister Rose at the time. Rose's husband, Jim, answered the phone, and I quickly told him, "I had an urgent feeling to call you right now. I feel Ryan! What's going on?"

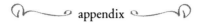 appendix

Jim answered, "They just found Ryan's body! Wait—how did you know?"

I explained to him what I had experienced and asked him to tell Mary Jane that I had called. I also told him that if Mary Jane would be up to it, I would be able to relay messages to her from her beloved son.

Within a short period of time, Mary Jane called me back and asked me to come right over. She confirmed that they had indeed found Ryan's body near a very long piece of driftwood on an island where the ocean meets the river. I hung up the phone and went right over to see her.

As soon as I arrived at Rose's house, I ran over to Mary Jane and gave her a big hug. I told her that Ryan wanted her to know what had happened to him. He said he had been at a party and then left to take a walk along the beach. When he was walking, he had accidentally fallen into the water, and eventually drowned. Mary Jane told me that all of this made sense; Ryan's friends had said that he was at a party with them right before his disappearance. The last thing he had told them was that he was going to walk along the beach to his girlfriend's house.

More than anything, Ryan wanted everyone to know that he was okay and was very sorry for what had happened. Because of the urgency of what he had to say, he was able to make himself loud and clear to me, so that I could easily relay what was needed to his beloved family. And, as I had requested of him earlier, he came to me right after his physical body was found.

Ryan has also communicated through me to his girlfriend, Nicole, to let her know that he is also around her and still loves her very much. Even though Nicole experienced the loss of her boyfriend's physical body, she knows that his beautiful soul continues to live on.

As for his family, they have since had many dreams and messages from their much-loved son, letting them know that he is with them. They are so happy to receive these constant reminders of his continued loving presence. Although his family misses him so much, they truly know that he is okay and is still watching over all of them.

Mother Reaches Out from the Other Side after Disappearing Many Years Earlier

Sometimes when I am doing a reading, I receive messages with random words, pictures, and names. I write them down, whether or not they mean anything, and the person can usually solve the pieces of

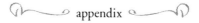

the puzzle from the reading at a later time. Shawn was truly thankful I had done this, when she found the random messages I had written down from a reading I had given her five years earlier. The Dewey Beach Police Department was actually using these notes as clues when they decided to reopen the case to find Shawn's beloved mother, who had been missing for a long time. Here are Shawn's words as she describes exactly what happened:

> My sister and I first met Karen Noe in 2002, almost nine years after our mother disappeared while on vacation in Dewey Beach, Delaware. Our family always felt an absolute knowingness that she died on the evening of her disappearance. Her body was never found, her missing person's case grew cold, and we were trying to accept that we might never know the answers to our agonizing questions regarding her death. On the advice of a friend, my sister and I arranged a session with Karen. Never could we have imagined how that brief meeting would affect our lives almost five years later.
>
> During our session on June 14, 2002, Karen was able to connect with a spirit who was giving her messages; she wrote random words on a small piece of paper that she had in front of her. The words didn't seem to make much sense to us at

173

the time, as we were hoping for a clear message from our mom that couldn't be disputed in our hearts. Suddenly, in the midst of writing, Karen reached for her throat and appeared to have trouble breathing. She apologized and told us she had to end the session. We knew that something was happening within her, and she appeared a bit frightened by it. We then told her that our mom was a missing person but that we truly believed she had died on the evening that she had disappeared.

Karen calmly asked us to return to her in a month, and she wouldn't accept any payment from us for her time. We drove home that day with a very strong intuition that it had been Mom speaking, but we didn't understand the messages. Later that day, I carefully placed Karen's notes in between the pages of a journal, where they would stay until March 28, 2007. I can't explain why we never returned to see Karen, except to simply say that it wasn't time—yet.

On March 11, 2007, we made our way back to Delaware for the first time in almost 14 years. It was a trip that we never could have imagined and never will forget. We had no intention of asking the Dewey Beach Police Department for any assistance, knowing that our mother's case had never been a priority for them in the first place.

appendix

We would do our own investigating, and we left a letter at the police station simply stating this fact.

As we drove through Dewey Beach that day, my sister and I kept seeing clear visuals of many of the random words that Karen had written so many years ago. We called home to a friend, Suzanne, who reminded us of our visit with the "angel lady" years before. (This is how we have always referred to Karen.) Our friend suggested that we look back through Karen's notes when we returned home.

The next day, we did read Karen's notes and realized that she had perfectly—and eerily—described the area in Delaware where our mom had disappeared. There was no denying this or the significance of the fact that Karen had truly communicated with our mom almost five years before.

Karen's notes led us back to Delaware a week later to continue our investigation, and led us to someone else who would affect our lives in a miraculous way. A young detective from Dewey Beach had received our note and asked if we would meet with him. It was out of simple courtesy that we agreed, but it was Divine Order that began to unfold around us. He reopened our mother's case—almost 14 years after her disappearance.

Some people would say that a million co-incidences led us to Karen, to Delaware, to this dedicated and caring detective. What we have learned along this journey is that there are no co-incidences, that everything has happened in the way, the time, and the order that it was always meant to happen.

Our realization of this didn't occur overnight. This has been an awakening that our mother has helped guide us—continues to guide us—through her ability to communicate with Karen.

The spiritual discoveries and experiences that have occurred throughout this investigation—this search for her remains, this journey for the truth—are so many for so very many people. It would take its own story to describe them all. I will try to make this as brief of a synopsis as possible.

"Tragic" is how my mom's death and disappearance had always been described—and felt—by all who loved her. At 53 years of age, it seemed that her life had been taken before it could possibly have been time. Without her body to properly bury, without answers to properly grieve over, nothing felt right or fair about the situation—not for our beautiful mother and not for those of us still living. Karen's gift of being able

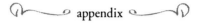

to communicate with her has changed that perception for all of us.

On March 28, 2007, at the urging of a friend, I decided to call Karen. I wasn't sure if she would remember our session from five years before, but I wanted to make her aware that she was already, unknowingly, helping with the investigation that had just been reopened.

That morning, two hours before I made the call, I broke down crying in front of my 17-year-old daughter. For the first time in years, I let her see the pain and anguish I was feeling about my mom. My daughter held me in her arms, while I repeated the same phrase over and over through gut-wrenching tears, "I have to find my mommy." The emotion of that exchange was huge, and I felt bad that she left for school that day having witnessed my breakdown. She sent me a text message shortly afterward to tell me she was worried about me—something she had never done before.

While sitting on my patio two hours later with my friend Suzanne, I picked up the phone and dialed Karen's number. The conversation that ensued truly felt as if the gates of heaven flew open. What I would soon learn was that the gates don't even exist; heaven's doorway is *always* open.

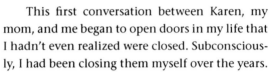

This first conversation between Karen, my mom, and me began to open doors in my life that I hadn't even realized were closed. Subconsciously, I had been closing them myself over the years.

Karen and I had just begun talking. She did remember meeting my sister and me in 2002. She suddenly interrupted our conversation and said there was someone trying to communicate with her. The words that then came from her mouth could only have come from the spirit world, from heaven, from my mom's spirit.

"Audrey," Karen said. "Your mom is worried about Audrey and says you need to talk to her." Audrey is my daughter's name. Audrey had tried to comfort me only hours before. I literally sank to my knees. Karen then said that my mom wanted me to know that she was with Annie Opal, my mom's sister, my aunt who had passed away five years before.

Karen and I spoke for almost two hours that day. The list of messages is long and miraculous, to say the least. There were so many personal truths that only my mom would know. There were descriptions of experiences that hadn't yet happened but have happened since. There were many clues about her missing person's case. There was also the first of what have turned out

to be many messages about the remains of her physical body.

In the beginning, we thought that she was leading us on a journey to find her remains, to find justice and closure. I began spending most of my time in Delaware, searching through the marshes for her bones—something physical and tangible that would certainly bring us the inner peace we so desired.

Each trip to Delaware became more and more remarkable, bringing another angel story, undeniable and amazing. These have been the most "real" experiences I have ever had. The angels make themselves clear and apparent, and their guidance is remarkable.

On April 26, 2007, Karen traveled to Delaware at the request of Detective Dempsey. The four of us spent the day together: Karen, the detective, my sister, and me. Our mom was there communicating through Karen every step of the way. Some of her messages were crystal clear; some of them we are still trying to figure out. She did allow us to ask questions about the case, but she was much more interested in talking about "personal stuff." She spoke a lot about the detective, telling us how highly she regarded him. She told us she had left her physical body at the time she was supposed to;

she hadn't been taken before she was ready. Karen relayed messages that touched all of our souls.

Out of all the incredible happenings of that day, the one that I cherish the most is a single word that my mom told Karen to say to me.

As I was drifting off to sleep in my hotel room the night before, I had asked my mom to please say something special for me. I had no idea if it was even possible to request this from a spirit, but I did so anyway.

At one point while Karen was receiving messages, she suddenly said she felt silly, but my mom wanted her to say something to me. Karen knew it had nothing to do with clues about the case. She then looked at me and simply said the word *elephant*. I began to cry and then to laugh. This was exactly what I had requested: simply the word *elephant*.

Karen's visit to Delaware was invaluable in many ways. Though we were not led to where our mother's remains are, we were led to the absolute conclusion that she did die there, that her spirit left her body on the evening she disappeared, and that she has been at peace ever since.

She does not desire for her body to be found, for she is no longer connected to it. When we try and explain to her that we need it to be found because we are still connected to the physical space

in which we live now, she reminds us that perhaps we should be more connected to the spiritual space in which we have always lived. So, she does help lead us—not to the discovery of her remains, but to the discovery of ourselves.

Karen has called me on several occasions over the past 18 months with messages from my mother. It's always out of the blue and always poignant. We have found her "random" words all over the place in Delaware. Our detective has sent us places while we were there, simply to get our minds off of digging through the marshlands, and Karen's clues were everywhere.

Karen once called to tell me that my mom had heard my prayers the night before, and she repeated them to me verbatim. She has also called before, during, and after huge events in our lives to tell us that our mom knows and is there with us. This is one of my favorite instances:

A week before my cousin David's wedding in Michigan on June 30, 2007, he called me to let me know that he had been thinking a lot about his Aunt Faye, my mom. He and his siblings had had a very close relationship with her since they were born.

David made a request of me that neither of us was sure was really possible, but I felt drawn to try. It was important to this young man, whom

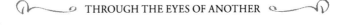

my mom had loved so much, that she somehow, in some way, make her spirit obvious at his wedding. He asked me if I would please ask her to be there. And I did ask—in a letter that I wrote to her just days before I left for Michigan with my sister and our children to attend the wedding. I asked that she bring a gift, in a grand fashion this time. I asked her to do something awesome—for David and for all of us who loved and missed her. I had no idea what she would come up with. On the day of the wedding, she would amaze and delight each and every one of us!

After the ceremony in the church, on our way to the reception, I suddenly felt a need to check my cell phone. There were three missed calls from Karen Noe! Her messages said that our mom had come through to her at four o'clock, telling her that she must call me at that very moment. The wedding began at four o'clock. I called her back immediately and left a message. Minutes later, waiting for the bride and groom to walk into the reception, Karen called again. My mom was there, Karen told us, and she was asking to speak with "David." With tears in my eyes from the joy in my heart, I ran to my cousin and handed him the phone. Because of Karen's gift, he was able to receive his Aunt Faye's gift.

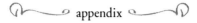

Our mother has continually told us that she is at peace and that our perception of justice is not what will bring us our peace. Where she now dwells, our human version of justice doesn't exist.

Karen has described our mom, her personality, exactly as she was. She has told us how strong willed our mother's spirit is: outgoing and charismatic, loving and humorous, sometimes demanding. Karen sees our mother's beauty without ever having known her in the physical world.

She and Karen, together, have truly brought us one of the most important messages we will ever receive, at least while here on Earth in human form:

Heaven is peace, peace is love, love is us.

Our Angels, the Universe, God, wish only for us to notice and experience the breathtaking beauty of life—both spiritual and physical—and to accept, to simply allow, that death of what is physical is inevitable. The death of the spirit is impossible.

Shawn's mom is still persistent in letting her family know that she is okay when she comes through at the most unexpected times. She doesn't want them to dwell on what she now knows to be insignificant—where her physical remains are. Instead, she wants everyone to truly understand that she is at peace and is still very much around her beautiful family.

Just as I was writing this chapter, the newspaper next to me literally flew off the table. As I went to pick it up, I wasn't at all surprised at the headline on the front page: "'Dewey' Is One of a Kind." Although the headline referred to a racehorse, I knew that Faye was giving yet one more message. The events that had occurred in Dewey Beach such a long time ago were one of a kind and, on the surface, a tragedy. Yet these very events are what brought her loving family and friends to the realization that the eternalness of one's soul is the most important concept of all.

Faye doesn't want her loved ones to grieve for her and keeps proving time and time again that she is still very much around them. She sees the bigger picture and doesn't want her family to focus on how she died or how to get back at the person who had killed her. As Shawn has stated so beautifully, her mother's most important message is that "our perception of justice is not what will bring us our peace. Where she now dwells, our human version of justice does not exist."

When a Child Crosses Over

Losing a child is unlike any other kind of grief. Parents somehow feel responsible, even though they are not. When a child comes through, I often see such relief from the parents when they become aware of the child's continued existence. Sometimes, when babies cross over, they are not yet able to come through on their own. In this case, other loved ones who have crossed over come through to let us know that the babies are with them. This happened when Kristy and Jon came in for a reading several years ago.

When this adorable couple came in, I wasn't sure what I was picking up on. I felt little energies, and interpreted them to be babies who were on the other side. I saw the number four, but I didn't understand what it meant. When I told them what I was feeling, they said they had lost quadruplets a few months earlier. As I was consoling them, reassuring them that the babies were okay, two more loved ones came through holding the babies; they gave me their names: Tom and Theresa. A smile appeared on Kristy's face when she confirmed that Tom and Theresa were her grandparents who had crossed over. Her grandparents had come to make sure Kristy and Jon knew that they were with the babies on the other side.

Kristy and Jon were relieved that their babies were okay and were with Kristy's loving family. After they left, I immediately knew that we would connect again, and we did indeed see each other a few times after that.

About a year later, Kristy had been trying to conceive once more, but to no avail; she had been disappointed each month when it didn't happen. One day as I was meditating, Kristy's deceased grandmother came to give me the message that Kristy was pregnant. I immediately called Kristy and asked her if she was expecting a baby. She said she didn't know, but was going to take a pregnancy test to find out.

As I was driving to get lunch later that day, a car cut me off. When I glanced at the license, it said "2 QUADS." As always, I don't believe in coincidences, and I knew this was a sign that two of her quadruplets were going to come back to her at this time.

Kristy called me back a few days later and confirmed what I already knew. She was ecstatic and was indeed "in the family way"!

And now for the happy ending: She has since given birth to adorable, healthy twins: Ryan and Casey. Both parents and babies are doing

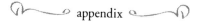

wonderfully, and I'm so thrilled that Kristy and Jon now have the family they had always wanted. They are all truly blessed!

⊡ ⊡ ⊡

An important fact is that children who have crossed over usually, but not always, grow on the other side. I have made this deduction after many readings in which children came through as the age they would have been, had they not died. However, the bottom line is this: they are *always* okay and want their parents to know that. Sometimes, although it's rare—as in the case of Kristy's twins— they may even decide to reincarnate right away to their loving parents. For the most part, though, after leaving this earth through physical death, souls typically wait for their immediate family to join them, and then they decide to return to earth all together.

When Someone Doesn't Know What a Message Means until Later

Once in a while, a loved one may come through with a message that a client does not understand. In my experience of doing readings, I still know that the message may be something significant, so

I write it down anyway. Such was the case in the following story.

As it is with almost everyone who makes an appointment, Pat came in with the intention of connecting with her deceased loved ones. The reading went well: her father, Martin, came through, and he showed me that he was "playing the spoons," just as he'd done when he was alive. Her brother Buddy came through too, and talked about events he was aware of that were happening with his family. However, at the end of the reading, he mentioned two unusual animals that left both Pat and me at a loss for words. He showed me a dog with an oxygen mask and a skunk. When I relayed these messages, Pat laughed and said she had no idea what they meant; I wrote them down anyway, just in case the messages would mean something in the future.

The very next day, I received a message on my answering machine from Pat, telling me to call her back because she had already found out what the messages meant. I called her back immediately and was anxious to hear what she had to say.

She said that after our reading, she had gone to a bridal shop to have a dress altered that she was going to wear to her daughter's wedding. When she arrived at the shop, the owner told her that she'd

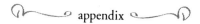

had a terrible week because of a bad fire in her house. After she was finished speaking, the woman's mother walked into the room and completed the story.

"Our dog had to receive oxygen," she said, "and he isn't doing very well."

Pat then continued and told me she had also spoken to her daughter right after our appointment. According to her daughter, on the day of our appointment, a skunk had hidden in her garage; it had become frightened and sprayed everything in the garage, including her car. Pat was telling me how upset her daughter was, because the awful odor just wouldn't go away, no matter what she did.

As Pat was speaking to me, I couldn't help but chuckle to myself, because the strange messages I had given to her the day before *did* turn out to be significant. I was so glad I'd been persistent and wrote them down, even though they didn't mean anything to Pat at the time.

Although Pat wasn't thrilled about her daughter's garage being sprayed by a skunk or the bridal-shop owner's dog needing an oxygen mask, she now knew without a doubt that her brother Buddy had been watching over his loved ones. She had proof that he was okay, through his confirming even the most unusual events that were happening around her and the family.

Connecting with Animals

I have been asked on many occasions whether animals can come through and give messages, and my answer is always the same: yes, they absolutely survive the physical body and are anxious to let you know they are all right. Many times they give their names, feelings, and pictures of things that were important to them. Even when the message is most unusual, I don't question whether or not to give it; I relay it anyway.

Such was the case for a wonderful couple from Virginia. When Joseph and Dorothy came in for a reading, their loved ones came through from the other side to speak to them. However, because it was so unusual, what stands out most in my mind from that reading was not a message from a person at all; it was from a grateful rodent!

As I was relaying messages to Joseph, a squirrel's spirit decided to appear and was insistent on thanking Joseph for saving his life. The squirrel showed me that Joseph had rescued him from a swimming pool and had given him mouth-to-mouth resuscitation.

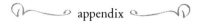

After relaying this to Joseph, he confirmed it all to be true. I was quite relieved, because I began to wonder if the information I was receiving was correct.

Because of this reading, I fully realize that animals are actually grateful for the loving things we do for them. They come through just as humans do to let us know they really do appreciate our random acts of kindness toward them.

❍ ❍ ❍

Just as I was writing this section on animals, a dog that had come through in a reading I gave a few months earlier decided to appear to me once again. Apparently, she wanted her story to be included in this book, so here it is.

When Roni came in for a reading, her adorable springer spaniel came through loud and clear to tell her owner that she was okay. She told me her name was Dora, and showed me that she had been hit by a car. She wanted her owners to know that if this accident hadn't occurred, another one would have, because it was time for her to leave her body. She didn't want her owners to feel guilty that they hadn't prevented her from running into the street, and she wanted to set the record straight. Dora wanted to take full responsibility for the accident and was sorry for the pain she had caused them all because of it. She even said that she would be coming back soon, and they would recognize her by her personality. Because of her strong willpower, I know she won't wait long to join her loving family once more.

Living Animals Can Give and Receive Messages, Too

I teach many workshops at my center, but one of my favorite classes of all time was one I gave on animal communication. Although there were a number of animals in the class that day, two clearly stand out in my mind: Darla, a very sweet cocker spaniel, and Zack, an adorable English springer spaniel.

I was sitting on one side of an L-shaped couch, teaching the course, and Darla and her owner, Carolyn, were on the other side. All of a sudden, Darla decided to walk toward me on the couch and gaze directly into my eyes as if she wanted to tell me something. At first, I didn't know if I was receiving the correct information from her. She relayed to me that she wasn't Darla anymore but was now "Thainy." When I repeated what I thought she had told me, Carolyn happily responded, "I knew it!"

Because I didn't understand this message, I asked Carolyn what it meant. According to Carolyn, Darla's

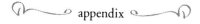

previous owners had abused her. For quite some time after Carolyn and her husband, John, had adopted her, Darla would just stay in the corner and never budge from that spot. Then, many months later, Darla's personality had suddenly changed for no apparent reason. Carolyn noticed this behavioral shift one day when Darla unexpectedly came out from the corner and decided to jump onto her lap. Ever since that incident, Carolyn noticed that Darla had begun to act a lot like Thainy, Carolyn and John's previous dog that had recently died.

So, the message the sweet cocker spaniel had given me that day during class certainly did make sense after all! Thainy's soul was now residing in Darla's body, and she was a "walk-in." And the best part is that this newfound information had confirmed what her owners had already suspected all along!

◙ ◙ ◙

In the beginning of the same class, I placed a dog biscuit in between the cushions next to me on the sofa. As I was doing this, Zack, an English springer spaniel, was sleeping comfortably on the floor on the other side of the room from where I was sitting.

About 45 minutes later, his owner, Tanis, wanted to see if we'd be able to send messages to Zack, even though he was still asleep. I told her that it was definitely possible, and asked each of the women in the class to send a beam of light from her heart chakra to Zack's. Then I told them to draw figure eights in the air toward Zack and visualize him waking up to get the treat.

After a few minutes of our trying to send him this message, Zack sat up from his slumber and looked at everyone as if to say, "All right, already, I'll listen to what you want me to do." To appease us, he walked directly to the treat without anyone showing him where it was. He then took the treat, ate it, strolled back to his original spot, plopped back onto his side, and immediately dozed off again.

Everyone in the class was amazed that they were actually able to successfully communicate telepathically with this beautiful dog. Of course, I already knew it was going to happen, and just smiled.

Loved Ones Helping from the Other Side

People who have crossed over often want to help loved ones who are still here on Earth, and they become frustrated when they are not being heard. The more important the message, the more persistent they will be in finding an avenue to "come through"

with what needs to be said. Such was the case with Tom, who decided to make his presence known during a class I was teaching.

After her friend's father had given her a copy of my first book, Theresa decided to take a class I was teaching on how to communicate with angels and deceased loved ones. Right in the middle of my class, her deceased father insisted on talking to her. He was so persistent that I had to stop teaching and announce that he was there. He first told me his name, Tom, and informed me that he had just recently crossed over. He asked me to tell Theresa and her sisters that he loved them very much and was around them. After I relayed a few more messages, Theresa wanted to know if she could ask him a question. I told her that she could try, but I didn't know for sure if he would answer it directly.

She then told me to ask him where the hidden money was. Apparently, her father had stored money somewhere in the house, and the family couldn't find it. They were ready to sell the house and needed to locate the money before they moved out.

In response to her question, Tom immediately showed me that it was under the pink insulation in the attic. Theresa told me the family had already looked everywhere, including the attic, but she was going to check it again.

Right after she went home, Theresa called me at my office. She was very excited and announced that she had indeed found a substantial amount of money in the attic under the insulation, just where her dad had said it would be. The family was able to breathe a sigh of relief and sell their house, grateful that the money their dad had intended for them was now in their hands. Not only was she given this monetary gift from the other side, but she also now had the wonderful knowledge that her dad was still very much around her and was watching over his loving family!

So Much More

I have shared these few stories in this appendix with the purpose of helping you to more fully understand what happens to your loved ones after they leave their physical bodies. There are so many more stories to tell, but that would be another book in itself. (If you are interested in reading more of these types of stories, you will be able to find them in my first book, *The Rainbow Follows the Storm: How to Obtain Inner Peace by Connecting with Angels and*

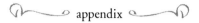

Deceased Loved Ones.) Simply understand that you are so much more than your physical body. Your true essence is energy, and this energy will never cease to exist. This is not something I *believe;* it is something I *know.* My wish is for *you* to know it too!

❀ ◉ ❀

acknowledgments

I wish to express my deepest appreciation to my family and friends, who have supported me on this spiritual journey. I love you all so much!

A special thanks to my soul mate, Ken, who makes me feel as if I'm the most important person in the world and who has continued to encourage me every step of the way. You are the gentlest, most caring person I have ever met, and I'm so blessed that you are in my life.

Extra hugs and blessings to my "angel friends," who always cheer me on and allow me to be myself. I feel as if I have known you all forever.

I am especially grateful to those of you whose stories are contained within these pages. Without you, there would be no book.

To those at Balboa Press, I am so appreciative for such an amazing experience prior to, during, and after the launch of the first printing of this book.

My deepest gratitude goes to Reid Tracy for believing in me. Thank you so much for your helpful advice while I was still at Balboa Press, and for granting me my lifelong dream of becoming a Hay House author.

To God and his many angels, who have always guided and protected me. Words cannot even begin to express my gratitude for your eternal presence!

And Mom, thank you for continuing to give me such amazing signs from heaven that let me know you are still watching over me. You were the best mother and friend anyone could ever have, and I'm so honored to have been your daughter. I will love you forever!

about the author

Karen Noe is a psychic medium and the author of *The Rainbow Follows the Storm: How to Obtain Inner Peace by Connecting with Angels and Deceased Loved Ones*. She is the founder of the Angel Quest Center in Ramsey, New Jersey, where she teaches classes, gives readings, and practices alternative healing. You can listen to Karen on *The Angel Quest Radio Show* by tuning to **www.wrcr.com** on the first Saturday of every month.

Please visit Karen's website: **www.karennoe.com**

❀ ◉ ❀

We hope you enjoyed this Hay House book.
If you'd like to receive our online catalog featuring
additional information on Hay House books and products,
or if you'd like to find out more about the
Hay Foundation, please contact:

Hay House, Inc., P.O. Box 5100, Carlsbad, CA 92018-5100
(760) 431-7695 or (800) 654-5126
(760) 431-6948 (fax) or (800) 650-5115 (fax)
www.hayhouse.com® • **www.hayfoundation.org**

▢ ▢ ▢

Published and distributed in Australia by:
Hay House Australia Pty. Ltd., 18/36 Ralph St.,
Alexandria NSW 2015 • *Phone:* 612-9669-4299 •
Fax: 612-9669-4144 • www.hayhouse.com.au

Published and distributed in the United Kingdom by:
Hay House UK, Ltd., 292B Kensal Rd., London W10 5BE • *Phone:*
44-20-8962-1230 • *Fax:* 44-20-8962-1239 • www.hayhouse.co.uk

Published and distributed in the Republic of South Africa by:
Hay House SA (Pty), Ltd., P.O. Box 990, Witkoppen 2068 •
Phone/Fax: 27-11-467-8904 • www.hayhouse.co.za

Published in India by:
Hay House Publishers India, Muskaan Complex, Plot No. 3,
B-2, Vasant Kunj, New Delhi 110 070 • *Phone:* 91-11-4176-1620 •
Fax: 91-11-4176-1630 • www.hayhouse.co.in

Distributed in Canada by:
Raincoast, 9050 Shaughnessy St., Vancouver, B.C. V6P 6E5 •
Phone: (604) 323-7100 • *Fax:* (604) 323-2600 • www.raincoast.com

▢ ▢ ▢

Take Your Soul on a Vacation

Visit **www.HealYourLife.com**® to regroup, recharge, and reconnect
with your own magnificence.Featuring blogs, mind-body-spirit news,
and life-changing wisdom from Louise Hay and friends.

Visit **www.HealYourLife.com** today!

Lightning Source UK Ltd.
Milton Keynes UK
UKOW051906170712

196143UK00002B/3/P